WHERE
GREAT WRITERS
GATHER

TREASURES OF THE BRITISH LIBRARY

文苑英华
来自大英图书馆的珍宝

上海图书馆　大英图书馆　编

SHANGHAI LIBRARY　　THE BRITISH LIBRARY

商务印书馆
创于1897　The Commercial Press

图书在版编目（CIP）数据

文苑英华：来自大英图书馆的珍宝/上海图书馆，
大英图书馆编.—北京：商务印书馆，2018

ISBN 978-7-100-15918-0

Ⅰ.①文… Ⅱ.①上… ②大… Ⅲ.①不列颠图书馆
—馆藏—图录 Ⅳ.① G259.561.6

中国版本图书馆 CIP 数据核字（2018）第 042455 号

文苑英华——来自大英图书馆的珍宝

上海图书馆　大英图书馆　编

商 务 印 书 馆 出 版
（北京王府井大街 36 号　邮政编码 100710）
商 务 印 书 馆 发 行
苏 州 市 越 洋 印 刷 有 限 公 司 印 刷
ISBN　978-7-100-15918-0

2018 年 3 月第 1 版　　　开本 787×1092　1/16
2018 年 3 月第 1 次印刷　印张 16.5

定价：128.00 元

本书总策划：周德明（Zhou Deming）

图录作者：
中方（以姓氏笔画为序）

　　刘明辉（Liu Minghui）　沈从文（Shen Congwen）　沙青青（Sha Qingqing）
英方

　　Alexandra Ault（亚历珊德拉·奥特）

———————————————

翻译：
中方（以姓氏笔画为序）

　　刘明辉（Liu Minghui）　沈从文（Shen Congwen）　周　庄（Zhou Zhuang）
英方（以姓氏笔画为序）

　　王　潭（Wang Tan）　朱　静（Zhu Jing）　孙小婷（Sun Xiaoting）

———————————————

专论中英文作者（以姓氏笔画为序）：

　　王　欣（Wang Xin）　刘立平（Liu Liping）　肖一之（Xiao Yizhi）

　　吴泽庆（Wu Zeqing）　吴　笛（Wu Di）

摄影：林　桦（Lin Hua）

篆刻：周建国（Zhou Jianguo）

版权声明 / Image Credits

  "文苑英华——来自大英图书馆的珍宝"是"大英图书馆在中国：共享知识与文化"双边文化交流项目中的重要展览，于2018年春在上海图书馆拉开序幕。这是中英两国高级别人文交流，也是上海图书馆和大英图书馆之间的第一次深度合作，更是两国人民之间的心灵互动。

  国之交在于民相亲，民相亲在于心相通。文学作品的译介是非常有效和重要的跨文化交流方式。众所周知，英国文学作品中的瑰宝灿若星河，是世界人民的共同财富，历来深受中国读者喜爱；中国翻译家和文学评论家的倾力译介，是文化交流中的有力推手，不断适应着人民日益增长的文化生活需要。

  文苑英华，美美与共；精神财富，互联互通。祝愿来自英国的珍宝在中国大地上继续枝繁叶茂，希冀中国的译介典籍在文化交流中永葆生机活力。

  有朋自远方来，不亦乐乎。我谨代表上海图书馆，热烈欢迎大英图书馆的来访，期待两馆的交流合作更加深入，共同铸就人类文明的新辉煌！

陈超

上海图书馆馆长
2018年元月

GREETINGS

In the spring of 2018, the exhibition 'Where Great Writers Gather: Treasures of the British Library' opens at Shanghai Library. This is an important exhibition in the bilateral cultural exchange program 'The British Library in China: Connecting through Culture and Learning'. Not only is it a high-level cultural exchange between China and the UK and the first extensive collaboration between Shanghai Library and the British Library, but also a spiritual interaction between the people of both countries.

The key to friendly relations between countries lies in the affinity between their people, which stems from mutual understanding. The translation of literary works is a very effective and important means of cross-cultural communication. As is known by all, the treasures of English literature are like brilliant stars in the sky, a wealth shared by people across the world and adored by Chinese readers. The dedication of Chinese translators and literary critics has given a powerful impetus to cultural exchanges and continuously fulfilled people's ever-increasing demand for cultural activities.

The finest of all blossoms from the garden of literature should grow together and reflect in and on one another's beauty, just as the spiritual and artistic wealth of nations should be interconnected and mutually appreciated. We hope that British blossoms continue to flourish in Chinese soil, and hope that the Chinese translation of English literary classics will forever retain its vitality.

As Confucius would say: It is always a great pleasure to receive friends from afar. On behalf of Shanghai Library, I heartily welcome the visit of our colleagues from the British Library and look forward to further cooperation between the two institutions. Together, we can contribute greatly to the prosperity of human civilisation.

Chen Chao
Director, Shanghai Library
January, 2018

GREETINGS ○

This exhibition celebrates five important British authors and unites two great institutions of literature and learning: the British Library and Shanghai Library. We are proud to be displaying original manuscripts by Charlotte Brontë, Charles Dickens, Percy Bysshe Shelley, T.S. Eliot and D.H. Lawrence as part of an exhibition looking at English literature within the context of translation and adaptation in China—and, more specifically, within Shanghai itself.

At the British Library, we hold one of the most important collections of unique literary manuscripts and highly-prized first editions created by world-famous authors. As part of our international purpose to 'work with partners around the world to advance knowledge and mutual understanding', I am delighted that we are collaborating with the remarkable Shanghai Library to display highlights from these wonderful archives, and learn more about our collections through exhibiting them to Chinese audiences.

This partnership with Shanghai Library is part of an ambitious three-year project— 'The British Library in China: connecting through culture and learning' —that aims to build closer cultural relations between the British Library and China, working with Chinese cultural and educational organisations. Funded by the UK Government, the project has seen us transform our engagement across China, developing exhibitions, online learning resources and a knowledge exchange programme. Sharing our most important literary icons with audiences in China is a symbol of our commitment to international partnership and dialogue, and I look forward to many more opportunities to share knowledge and collections in the future.

Roly Keating

Chief Executive, The British Library

January, 2018

寄语

本展览联合大英图书馆与上海图书馆这两大久负盛名的文化与研究机构，隆重展出夏洛蒂·勃朗特、查尔斯·狄更斯、珀西·比希·雪莱、T.S. 艾略特、D.H. 劳伦斯五位英国文豪的手稿。此次展览在文学译介、改编史的语境下重新审视英国文学原著，并探究、呈现英国文学是如何通过其中文译著、编著与上海这座城市产生共鸣。

大英图书馆藏有世界文学巨擘独一无二的手稿，及珍贵的初版书籍。秉持着大英图书馆的国际宗旨"与世界各地的合作伙伴一起推动知识传播，增进文化间的相互理解"，我们十分荣幸能与上海图书馆联袂，在全新的语境下呈现我馆所藏瑰宝，并愿借此展览同中国观众相互加深理解，共享文学的奥妙。

我们与上海图书馆的此次合作是大英图书馆一项为期三年的宏大项目"大英图书馆在中国：共享知识与文化"的一部分。该项目旨在与中国文化、教育机构合作，加深大英图书馆与中国的文化交流。在英国政府的资助下，我们通过这个项目开辟出与中国伙伴机构合作的全新模式，包括策划展览、开发线上学习资源，推出专业人员交流互访计划等。我们秉承国际合作、全球对话的理念，为中国观众呈现我们最为珍贵的文学瑰宝，并期待在未来能够有更多机会共享知识与馆藏。

罗伊·基廷

大英图书馆首席执行官

2018年元月

西方文学作品在中国的翻译是中西文化交流的产物，其始于明末传教士的在华译述，继之于中国译者的踵事增华。学界一般以明天启五年（1625）在西安出版的由金尼阁（Nicolas Trigault, 1577～1628）口授，张庚笔传的伊索寓言《况义》为其开端。第一首汉译英诗《圣梦歌》（Visio Sancti Bernardi）也早在明末（1637）由传教士艾儒略（Guilio Aleni, 1582～1649）译出。之后数百年，西方文学随着西学的东传，从零篇短章，历经晚清和"五四"以来的大量翻译、出版与研究，成为广大中国读者喜闻乐见的文学作品。英国文学是我国翻译时间早且数量众多的对象之一，其作品深受中国译者的重视和读者的喜爱。英国文学为影响中国现代文学创作，开拓中国读者的文学视野，增进中英两国之间知识与文化的共享，提供了丰盛的资源。

上海具有海纳百川的历史传统，是中西文化交流先驱徐光启的故乡。自晚清以来，上海开风气之先，成为融汇中外文明的枢纽，是中国翻译出版英国文学的主要中心，在英国文学的推介中发挥了重要作用。现有资料表明，我国近代外国小说的翻译发轫于英国小说，始见于上海的报刊。如1872年5月21日至24日的《申报》连载了英国小说家斯威夫特（Jonathan Swift）的《格列佛游记》（Gulliver's Travels）中"小人国"部分的译文，约五千字，名为《谈瀛小录》；1872年5月31日起分六期刊登的《乃苏国奇遇》是英国小说家马里亚特（Frederick

Marryat）的《听很多故事的把沙》（*The Pacha of Many Tales*）中的《希腊奴隶的故事》（*Story of the Greek Slave*）的译文。1873 年 1 月，申报馆出版的《瀛寰琐记》第 3 期上发表了中国第一部汉译小说《昕夕闲谈》，共连载 26 期，约 30 万字。时过百年，经美国学者韩南研究，此书原著是英国作家爱德华·布尔沃·利顿（Edward Bulwer Lytton）所作的《夜与昼》（*Night and Morning*）。以上汉译文献在上海图书馆均有实物收藏，见证了英国文学在上海的早期传播历史。此外，英国 19 世纪的伟大作家狄更斯与上海也有跨越时空的缘分，他的一本个人藏书神奇地收藏在上海图书馆，令人抚书遐想，肃然起敬。

上海作为中国近现代文化重镇，发达的新闻出版业为人文荟萃的上海知识分子提供了广阔的活动舞台，有力地促进了外国文学的译介，为中国的新文学成长输送了丰富的养料。20 世纪上半期的上海，集聚了我国优秀的翻译与编辑群体，以报刊和图书为媒介，大量外国文学作品在此纷纷发表，占据了中国翻译出版的半壁江山。上海的许多期刊不仅辟出专栏发表译作，还出版了多种翻译专号或纪念专号、专栏，以英国作家数量居多。如《创造季刊》（1923 年 9 月 10 日 1 卷 4 期）的"雪莱纪念栏"，《小说月刊》（1924 年 4 月 10 日 15 卷 4 号）的"拜伦专辑"，《现代》（1932 年 12 月 1 日 2 卷 2 期）的"约翰·高尔斯华绥特辑"，《译文》（1937 年 3 月 16 日 1 卷 1 期）的"迭更司特辑"，《新演剧》（1937 年 6 月 5 日 1 卷 1 期）的"莎士比亚特辑"等。以商务印书馆为首的上海出版机构在译介外国文学方面做出了重大的贡献。除了人们熟知的商务版早期的《说部丛书》和从中抽印汇编的《林译小说》中有史蒂文森、司各特、笛福、斯威夫特、莎士比亚、狄更斯等多位英国作家外，当时的许多文学译作丛书也为中国读者传递了丰富多彩的英国文学。兹以上海图书馆所编《中国近代现代丛书目录总目》中著名译文丛书为例，英国文学作品数量居于前茅，如商务印书馆 1928 年 4 月至 1950 年 2 月出版的《世界文学名著丛书》共 154 种，其中英国 28 种；启明书局 1931 年 8 月至 1949 年 5 月出版的《世界文学名著丛书》共 78 种，其中英国 22 种；中华书局 1939 年 8 月至 1947 年 10 月出版的《世界少年文学丛书》共 8

种，英国占了7种；世界书局1931年10月至1937年3月出版的《世界少年文库》共编号47种（缺7种），英国13种。在大型综合性丛书《万有文库》所选的文学译作中，第1集33种中有英国作品8种，第2集46种中有英国作品9种。由此可见，英国文学作品的译介在上海深受欢迎，而且许多英国文学的名家名作在上海得到了首译首印，多位作家的名作被一书多译，多种作品在沪成为名译佳作，数十年后仍令人称道。据国家版本图书馆编《1949～1979翻译出版外国古典文学著作目录》统计，我国大陆地区在此30年间翻译出版了47个国家276位作家的1250多部外国古典文学作品，在上海出版的就有710种，占全国的半数以上，其中英国文学仍有较高的比例。中国改革开放初期，在全国形成了争相购阅外国文学名著热的景象，重印和新译的英国文学作品纷纷问世。上海的翻译家和出版界近40年来不断努力，推出了一系列英国作家名著，如19卷的《狄更斯文集》，5卷本的《艾略特文集》等，从古典到当代，各类译作琳琅满目，读者受益无穷。

19世纪中叶以来，上海是我国西学人才的集聚之地，涌现了众多著名的翻译家，其中不少人身兼作家、学者和编辑，在推动外国文学传播方面具有综合优势。他们的翻译成果见证了上海从传教士和外国人，或"口授笔录"的中外合作到由中国人用中文翻译的转折。我们从那些传世百年的文学译作中，可以看到文本的呈现形式经历了译述、归化、文言到白话文的升华，从中展现了文学译介在社会环境和文化语境影响下的变迁。外国文学的译介为促进中国的文学创作手法、叙事方式和艺术表现发挥了重要作用，助推了文学观念的变革和文学思潮的兴起，为中国20世纪的文学发展提供了典范文本，极大地丰富了中国读者的文学欣赏与阅读。英国文学作品是这一过程中的重要媒介和内容。

虽然我们从英国文学作品在华传播史上可以看到大量在沪出版的翻译作品，但雪莱、夏洛蒂·勃朗特、狄更斯、D.H.劳伦斯、T.S.艾略特五位英国作家的手稿首次集中亮相于上海，是一个十分难得的历史时刻。大英图书馆提供的珍贵手稿，让我们从笔底波澜中亲沐手泽，倾听大师的心声，体验隐匿于文字背影中的创作艰辛，通过五位作家作品在中国传播与接受的历史，从名作名译中含英咀华，认知中英文化交流的互学互鉴与融合，以更大的热情学习和吸收人类文明的优秀成果。

　　本书是上海图书馆和大英图书馆为"文苑英华——来自大英图书馆的珍宝"展而共同编著的图录，全书以英国作家手稿为中心，辅之以上海图书馆所藏的相关文献，旨在纪念和见证中英双方合作的展览成果，通过此书将珍贵的文献长存于读者的记忆中，成为永不落幕的纸上展览，固化双方的友谊。在此感谢中英双方参与人员为此书的编写、翻译和出版所付出的热情与劳动。

编　者

2018 年 2 月 23 日于上海图书馆

目 录
CONTENTS

...med you left, Envy would kill

...re, & leave to Wonder & Despair

...nistration of the thoughts that fill

...ind, which, like a worm whose life may

...on of the Unapproachable.

...your creations rise as fast & fair

...ct worlds at the creators will,

...bows itself before the godhead there

...h is my regard, that, not your fa...

...on the present by the coming ho...

...well-won prosperity & power

...e regret for his unhonoured na...

...ares these words.— The ...... beneath

...lift itself in worship to the Go...

I

珀西·比希·雪莱

PERCY
BYSSHE
SHELLEY

Portrait of Percy Bysshe Shelley, frontispiece to *The Poetical Works of Percy Bysshe Shelley*, edited by Mrs Shelley (London: E. Moxon, 1839), British Library W6/9198 DSC.

珀西·比希·雪莱肖像,《珀西·比希·雪莱诗选》卷首插图。玛丽·雪莱编《珀西·比希·雪莱诗选》(伦敦: E. 莫克森出版社,1839 年)。大英图书馆藏: W6/9198 DSC.

珀西·比希·雪莱 是英国最伟大的浪漫主义诗人之一。1792 年
8 月 4 日，他出生于英国萨塞克斯郡一个贵族地主家庭，自幼好学深思，少年时
代就已展现出反抗精神。1810 年出版小说《扎斯特洛齐》及最早的两本诗集。
1811 年 3 月，雪莱因发表小册子《论无神论的必要性》，被牛津大学开除。8 月，
他与 16 岁的哈丽艾特·威斯布鲁克私奔结婚。1812 年，雪莱开始与激进思想家
威廉·戈德温交往，动笔写作第一部重要长诗《麦布女王》(1813)。1814 年，雪
莱与戈德温之女玛丽 (1797 ~ 1851) 私奔。1816 年哈丽艾特自杀，雪莱与玛丽
正式结婚。在此期间，雪莱遍游法、意、瑞士等国，与因不见容于英国社会而
去国离乡的另一位浪漫主义大诗人拜伦 (1788 ~ 1824) 结为挚友。1818 年，雪
莱携妻儿前往意大利，自此进入创作高峰期，先后完成长诗《伊斯兰的起义》
(1818)、诗剧《解放了的普罗米修斯》(1820)、诗体悲剧《钦契》(1819)、政治
讽刺诗《暴政的假面游行》(1819)、哀悼诗人济慈的长诗《阿多尼斯》(1821)、
歌颂希腊独立革命的诗剧《希腊》(1822) 以及《西风颂》(1819) 等大量抒情诗，
还撰写了文论名篇《诗辩》(1821)。1822 年 7 月 8 日，雪莱驾驶的帆船"爱丽
儿"号在意大利斯佩齐亚湾遇风暴沉没，他的遗体数日后才被发现，火化后安
葬于罗马新教徒墓地。玛丽·雪莱为亡夫亲拟了拉丁文墓志铭"众心之心"(Cor
cordium)，她毕生致力于整理出版雪莱遗著，自己也是一位颇有成就的作家，其
长篇小说《弗兰肯斯坦》(1818) 影响尤为深远。

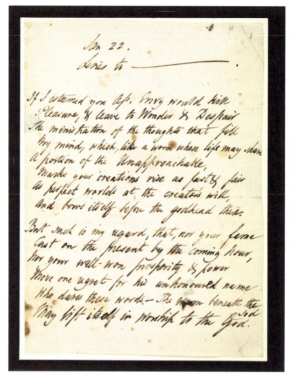

Manuscript of 'Sonnet to Byron' by Percy Bysshe Shelley, about 1821–22, British Library Zweig MS 188.

《致拜伦的十四行诗》手稿，珀西·比希·雪莱作，约 1821 年至 1822 年。大英图书馆藏：Zweig MS 188.

This small manuscript by Percy Bysshe Shelley (1792–1822) is titled 'Lines to _____' but is better known as 'Sonnet to Byron', and was probably written in late 1821 or early 1822. The subject of the 14-line, two stanza sonnet was not publicly identified until 1833 by the poet and cousin of

珀西·比希·雪莱（1792 ～ 1822）的这份小型手稿约作于 1821 年末或 1822 年初，题为《致 _____》，但《致拜伦的十四行诗》这一标题更广为人知。然而直到 1833 年，这篇双节十四行诗才由雪莱的表兄、诗人托马斯·麦德温鉴定为出

Frontispiece to *The Poetical Works of Percy Bysshe Shelley* (London: W. Dugdale, 1839), British Library 11612.b.30.

《珀西·比希·雪莱诗选》卷首插画（伦敦：W. 达格代尔出版社，1839 年）。大英图书馆藏：11612.b.30.

Shelley, Thomas Medwin. The poem is a tribute to Lord Byron's genius while also an admission of Shelley's own sense of inferiority. It begins 'If I esteemed you less, Envy would kill' and ends 'The worm beneath the sod / May lift itself in worship to the God'. Byron and Shelley first met in 1816 and rented houses near each other by the shore of Lake Geneva, Switzerland. It was during this trip that Mary Wollstonecraft Godwin, who was to later marry Shelley, was inspired to write the famous novel *Frankenstein*. On this same trip, Percy Shelley wrote *Hymn to Intellectual Beauty* after a boating tour with Byron. **[Fig. 1]**

自雪莱之笔。这篇诗作表达了诗人对拜伦勋爵才华的崇敬之情，同时也体现出诗人自愧不如的情感。该诗以"我若不是这样钦佩你，忌妒便会 / 败坏喜悦"[1] 开篇，以"虫豸 / 也能由于崇敬上帝而从泥土升起"[2] 作结。拜伦与雪莱初识于 1816 年，因为二人在瑞士旅行时恰巧租住在日内瓦湖边相邻的房子。也正是在这次旅行中，雪莱未来的妻子玛丽·沃斯通克拉夫特·戈德温产生了著名科幻小说《弗兰肯斯坦》的创作灵感，而雪莱在一次与拜伦的泛舟之游后，创作了《赞智力之美》。（图 1）

'Sonnet to Byron' was written only a few months before Shelley died in July 1822. The first seven lines of the poem were first published by Thomas Medwin in his 'Memoir of Shelley' in the *Athenaeum* magazine in 1832. Shelley composed another poem about Byron in around 1818 after Shelley had renewed contact with the poet in Venice, Italy: 'O mighty mind, in whose deep stream this age Shakes like a reed in the unheeding storm, Why dost thou curb not thine own sacred rage?'. This and the Sonnet demonstrate a sustained admiration of Byron's abilities. The manuscript is on a single sheet of paper whose edges have been cut down. It bears evidence of vertical folding, suggesting it was transported in a small notebook or pocket.

雪莱于 1822 年 7 月去世,《致拜伦的十四行诗》完成于他去世的几个月前。诗的前七行最早出现在托马斯·麦德温于 1832 年为《雅典娜神殿》杂志所写的《纪念雪莱》一文中。雪莱于 1818 年前后写过另一首关于拜伦的诗,作于诗人在意大利威尼斯与拜伦再次相见之后:"哦,伟大的心灵,在这心灵深沉的激流中,整个时代战栗了,似芦苇面临无情的暴风,究竟是为了什么,抑制不住你神圣的激愤?"这首诗以及《致拜伦的十四行诗》体现出雪莱一直以来对拜伦的才能的钦佩。《致拜伦的十四行诗》的手稿写在一张被裁过边的纸上,纸上留有纵向折叠的痕迹,表明有人曾将它折叠起来夹在小笔记本里或装在口袋里携带。

Fig.2

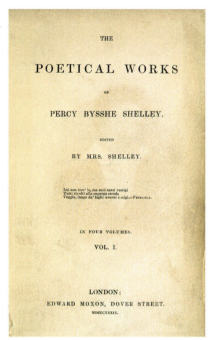

Title page of Frontispiece to *The Poetical Works of Percy Bysshe Shelley* (London: E. Moxon, 1839), British Library 1611.df.18.

《珀西・比希・雪莱诗选》卷首扉页（伦敦：E. 莫克森出版社，1839 年）。大英图书馆藏：1611.df.18.

The manuscript was owned by Mary Shelley, who after copying it gave it to her friend Charlotte Murchison sometime between 1831 and 1833. It was sold at Sotheby's Auctioneers on 16 December 1931 (lot 713) by Sir Kenneth Murchison and purchased by the manuscript collector Stefan Zweig. The Trustees of Stefan Zweig presented this manuscript and the Zweig Collection to the British Library in 1986. The Stefan Zweig collection is one of the most important collections of literary, historical and musical manuscripts amassed in the 20th century. **[Fig. 2]**

玛丽・雪莱曾是这份手稿的拥有者。1831 年到 1833 年之间，她将手稿抄写过后，将手稿赠与友人夏洛特・默奇森。在 1931 年 12 月 16 日苏富比的拍卖会上，肯尼斯・默奇森爵士将手稿拍卖（拍品号 713），由作家、手稿收藏家斯蒂芬・茨威格购得。1986 年，斯蒂芬・茨威格的受托人将这份手稿以及茨威格的其他藏品赠予大英图书馆。斯蒂芬・茨威格对文学、历史与乐谱手稿的收藏是 20 世纪该门类最权威、最重要的组成部分之一。（图 2）

1　珀西・比希・雪莱《雪莱抒情诗选》，江枫译，湖南文艺出版社，1996 年，第 251 页。
2　同上，第 115 页。

雪莱作品在中国
Percy Bysshe Shelley's works in China

  雪莱是在中国译介最早、影响最大的英国浪漫主义诗人之一。早在 20 世纪初，他的事迹、作品就已经被介绍到中国。到"五四"时期之后，雪莱的坎坷生平、反抗精神和杰出诗艺更是引起了文学界乃至广大新一代青年知识分子的广泛共鸣，几乎成为一个时代的偶像，译介、评论层出不穷，对中国新诗的发展也产生了相当的影响。20 世纪五六十年代，对雪莱的译介、评论虽不可避免地受到时代因素的一定影响，却依然颇为繁荣。20 世纪 80 年代开始至今，对雪莱作品的译介、研究出现了又一次高潮，达到了前所未有的广度和深度。

作品译介
Translations

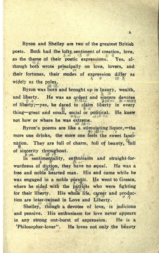

师梨（雪莱）《冬日》，《潮音》，苏曼殊编译，湖畔诗社重印，1925 年。
'Winter' (A Song；'A widow bird sate mourning for her love...'), trans. by Mandju (Su Manshu), reprinted in *Chao Yin* (A selection of poems by Byron, Shelley, Burns and others), Lake Poets' Society, 1925.

  早在 20 世纪初，著名诗人苏曼殊（1884～1918）就将雪莱短诗《冬日》[1] 译成汉文五言古诗，并附载雪莱的另一首名作《爱的哲学》原文，和此前同样用旧体诗体裁译出的拜伦《去国行》（ *My Native Land — Good Night* ）、《大海》（ *The Ocean* ）、《留别雅典女郎》（ *Maid of Athens，ere We Part* ）、《哀希腊》（ *The Isles of Greece* ），彭斯《颖颖赤墙靡》（ *A Red，Red Rose* ）等诗一同收入自己编译的《潮音》一书，前附英国友人佛莱蕉（ W.J.B. Fletcher ）序（英文）、苏曼殊 1906 年所作《拜轮诗选》序（中文，末原署"光绪三十二年"，后改作"戊申"）及 1909 年作《潮音》自序（英文）。此后书中的拜伦诗又曾以《拜轮诗选》之名出版单行本。

---

1 原为未完成的诗剧《查理一世》（ *Charles the First* ）中弄臣阿奇（ Archy ）所唱的歌。

《云之自质》，叶中泠译，《华侨杂志》第二期，1913 年。
'The Cloud', trans. by Ye Zhongling (Ye Yusen), *The Chinese Overseas Magazine*, No. 2, 1913.

　　1913 年，学者、诗人叶玉森（号中泠，1880 ～ 1933）以骚体译出了雪莱的名篇《云》，刊登于《华侨杂志》第二期。同期还发表了他分别以古乐府体、四言诗体译出的另两首诗作：滕蒲孙（今译丁尼生）《战死者之孀与孤》（ *The Widow and the Child*)、龙斐罗（今译朗费罗）《矢与歌》（ *The Arrow and the Song*)。

《南社诗录：译英吉利诗人锡兰情诗四解》，杨铨译，
《南社》第十一期，1914 年。
'Love's Philosophy', trans. by Yang Quan（Yang Xingfo）, *Nan She*, Vol. 11, 1914.

　　1914 年，著名学者、社会活动家杨铨（号杏佛，1893～1933）以类似六朝民歌的五言诗体翻译了雪莱《爱的哲学》，题为《译英吉利诗人锡兰情诗四解》，发表于《南社》第十一期。1933 年杨杏佛遭国民党特务暗杀后，《人间世》杂志 1934 年第十一期再次发表这首译诗以示纪念。1940 年《沙漠画报》第三卷第十四期也转载了这首译诗，改题《英国情诗四节》，未署译者姓名。

　　随着新文学运动的兴起，雪莱作品的汉译逐渐从文言传统诗体转向白话新诗体。如郭沫若在 1920 年 3 月 3 日致宗白华的信中，仍用传统五言诗翻译了"雪诔"《百灵鸟曲》（后改题《云鸟曲》，即雪莱《云雀颂》）。1923 年 9 月，《创造季刊》特辟"雪莱纪念栏"，发表了郭沫若翻译的《雪莱的诗》，并附成仿吾译《哀歌》及译序、年谱。1926 年由上海泰东图书局出版单行本《雪莱诗选》。其中《转徙》、《招"不幸"辞》（*Invocation to Misery*）等篇仍用五言诗、骚体等传统诗体翻译，但《西风颂》（*Ode to the West Wind*）等多数诗作译文已用白话自由诗体。郭沫若在译序中自称"我爱雪莱，我能感听得他的心声"，"我译他的诗，便如我自己在创作的一样"，认为作诗译诗不必拘泥于"文言白话，韵体散体"等形式。然而如《西风颂》原文使用了严谨的三韵句（terza rima）格律，同时多用戏剧化的跨行句法，既有建筑般的严整，又环环相扣、一气呵成，这在自由体的译文中却难以传达了。

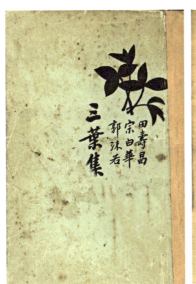

《百灵鸟曲》，郭沫若译，收入田寿昌、宗白华、郭沫若《三叶集》，亚东图书馆，1920 年。
'To a Skylark', trans. by Guo Moruo, in *Kleeblatt* (*Clover*) by Tian Shouchang, Zong Baihua and Guo Moruo, Ya Dong Book Company, 1920.

《雪莱的诗》，郭沫若、成仿吾译，《创造季刊》第一卷第四期，1923 年。
'Shelley's Poems', trans. by Guo Moruo, and Cheng Fangwu, *Chuang Zao Ji Kan* (*Creation Quarterly*), Vol. 1, No. 4, 1923.

《雪莱诗选》，郭沫若译编，泰东图书局，1926 年。
Selected Poems of Shelley, trans. by Guo Moruo and Cheng Fangwu, Tai Dong Book Company, 1926.

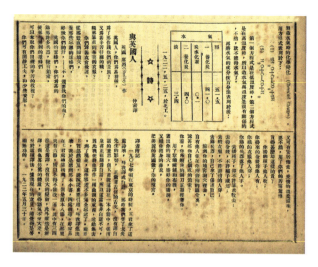

《与英国人》，仲密（周作人）译，《晨报副刊》1922 年 5 月 31 日。

'Men of England', trans. by Zhou Zuoren, *Chen Bao Fu Kan*, May 31, 1922.

《爱》，朱湘译，《小说月报》第十七卷第六期，1926 年。

'One Word Is Too Often Profaned', trans. by Zhu Xiang, *The Short Story Magazine*, Vol. 17, No. 6, 1926.

《诗一首》，胡适译，《新星》创刊号，1935 年。

'Music, When Soft Voices Die', trans. by Hu Shi, *Nova*, No. 1, 1935.

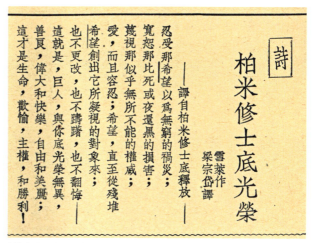

《柏米修士底光荣》，梁宗岱译，《人间世》1935 年第 21 期。
'To suffer woes which Hope thinks infinite' from *Prometheus Unbound*, trans. by Liang Zongdai, *Ren Jian Shi*, No. 21, 1935.

《雪莱诗钞》，郭蕊、吴兴华、宋悌芬译《西洋文学》
1940 年第 2 期。
'A Selection of Shelley's Poems', trans. by Guo Rui, Wu Xinghua and Song Tifen, *Western Literature*, No. 2, 1940.

　　20 世纪 20 至 40 年代，雪莱诗作的译文常见于各种报刊，总体数量难以统计，译者还包括了胡适、周作人、郑振铎等著名学者、作家以及诗人朱湘、宋悌芬等。

《西风颂》的几种译文
Several Chinese versions of *Ode to the West Wind*

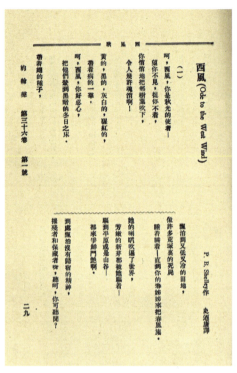

《西风辞》，田世昌译，《国学丛刊》
第二卷第一期，1924 年。
Trans. by Tian Shichang, *Guo Xue Cong Kan* (*Miscellanies of Traditional Chinese Studies*), Vol. 2, No. 1, 1924.

《西风》，史迺康译，《约翰声》第三十六卷第一期，
1924 年。
Trans. by Shi Naikang, *The St. John's Echo*, Vol. 36, No. 1, 1924.

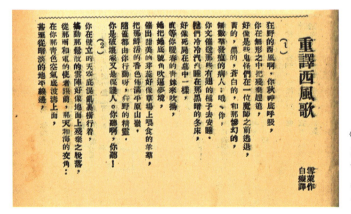

《重译西风歌》，白痴译，《大夏周刊》第
五十九期，1928 年。
Trans. by 'Bai Chi' ('Idiot'), *The Great China University Weekly*, No. 59, 1928.

《西风歌》，涧漪译，《朝华》第一卷第一期，1929 年。
Trans. by Jian Yi, *Zhao Hua* (*Morning Flowers*), Vol. 1,
No. 1, 1929.

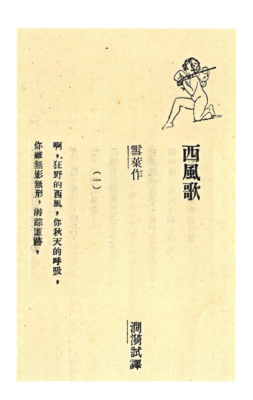

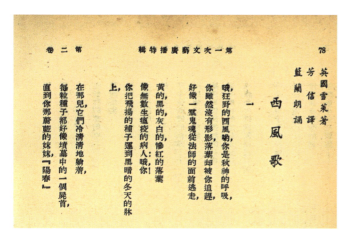

《西风歌》，芳信译，《大陆》第二卷第三期，1941 年。
Trans. by Fang Xin, *Da Lu* (*Continent*), Vol. 2, No. 3, 1941.

　　总的来说，这一时期雪莱作品译文虽多，但选目主要集中于《西风颂》《云》等若干抒情诗名篇，仅《西风颂》译文就至少有十余种之多。

《诗辩》，伍蠡甫译，商务印书馆，1937 年。
A Defence of Poetry, trans. by Woo Lifu,
the Commercial Press, 1937.

1820 年，雪莱的好友皮可克（T.L. Peacock）发表《诗之四阶段》，认为诗歌在近代文明社会中已经是过时之物。雪莱为反驳此文，撰写了长篇论文《诗辩》，成为西方文论史上的经典名篇。1937 年初，伍蠡甫译《诗辩》由商务印书馆出版，还附有详细的译注与皮可克《诗之四阶段》译文，标志着中国的雪莱译介已经开始进入更为严谨而学术化的阶段。

《明天：雪莱抒情诗选》，徐迟译，雅典书屋，1943 年。
Tomorrow：*Selected Lyric Poems of Shelley*, trans. by Xu Chi, Ya Dian Book Company, 1943.

20 世纪 40 年代，在抗战与内战的烽火中，雪莱作品的译介仍在继续，在广度和深度上都比此前有所拓展，译文质量也有了长足的进步。如著名作家徐迟（1914～1996）译雪莱诗选《明天》不仅选译了《西风歌》《云》《云雀颂》等此前已多次被译介的抒情名篇，还收录了如《赞知性的美》这样题旨颇为抽象的哲理诗及《敏感树》这样主题较为隐晦的诗篇；译文在意义、韵律等方面都较为忠实原文，末附长篇后记《雪莱欣赏》，标志着译者对雪莱作品的理解、研究已经较为深入。

《解放了的普罗米修斯》(四幕诗剧)，方然译，雅典书屋，
1944 年。
Prometheus Unbound, trans. by Fang Ran, Ya Dian Book
Company, 1944.

《沈茜》(五幕悲剧)，方然译，新地出版社，1944 年。
The Cenci, trans. by Fang Ran, Xin Di Press,
1944.

　　1944 年，方然翻译的诗剧《解放了的普罗米修斯》同样由桂林雅典书屋出版。这部诗剧
借用古希腊神话主题，表现代表暴力、威权、黑暗的邱比特（朱庇特）最终失败，代表光明、
自由、正义的普罗米修斯乃至整个世界都得以解放，富于乐观精神和哲理意味。译文后附注释
及缪灵珠的评析文章《〈解放了的普罗米修斯〉之时代意义》。方然还翻译了雪莱的另一出著名
诗剧《沈茜》(《钦契》)，也在同年出版。

《解放了的普罗密修斯》，邵洵美译，人民文学出版社，
1957 年。
Prometheus Unbound, trans. by Shao Xunmei,
People's Literature Publishing House, 1957.

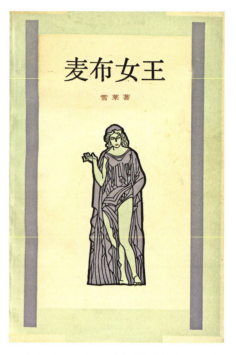

《麦布女王》，邵洵美译，上海译文出版社，1983 年。
Queen Mab, trans. by Shao Xunmei, Shanghai
Translation Publishing House, 1983.

《雪莱抒情诗选》，查良铮译，人民文学出版社，
1958 年。
Selected Lyric Poems of Shelley, trans.
by Zha Liangzheng, People's Literature
Publishing House, 1958.

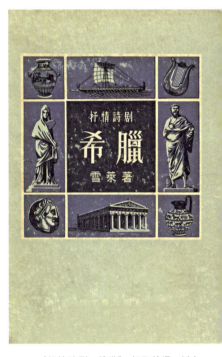

《伊斯兰的起义》，王科一译，上海文艺
出版社，1962年。
The Revolt of Islam, trans. by Wang
Keyi, Shanghai Literature and Arts
Press, 1962.

《钦契》，汤永宽译，上海文艺出版社，
1962年。
The Cenci, trans. by Tang Yongkuan,
Shanghai Literature and Arts Press,
1962.

《抒情诗剧：希腊》，杨熙龄译，新文
艺出版社，1957年。
Hellas, trans. by Yang Xiling, New
Literature and Arts Press, 1957.

　　20世纪五六十年代，由于雪莱的进步思想和革命精神，再加上他曾经得到马克思、恩格斯的高度评价，雪莱成为最受重视的西方诗人之一，作品译介进入了新的高潮。尤其是邵洵美、查良铮（穆旦）等杰出诗人的参与，使得这一时期的翻译达到了前所未有的高度。

《雪莱抒情诗选》，杨熙龄译，上海译文出版社，1981 年。
Selected Lyric Poems of Shelley, trans. by Yang Xiling, Shanghai Translation Publishing House, 1981.

《雪莱政治论文选》，杨熙龄译，商务印书馆，1981 年。
Political Essays of Shelley, trans. by Yang Xiling, the Commercial Press, 1981.

《雪莱诗选》，江枫译，湖南人民出版社，1980 年。
Selected Poems of Shelley, trans. by Jiang Feng, Hunan People's Publishing House, 1980.

《雪莱全集》(七卷本)，江枫译，河北教育出版社，2000 ～ 2001 年。
Complete Works of Shelley (7 Vols), trans. by Jiang Feng, Hebei Education Publishing House, 2000-01.

改革开放时期，雪莱作品的译介比此前任何时期都更为繁荣，各种译本陆续出现。在众多译者中，以江枫的贡献最大。2000 年至 2001 年，他翻译的七卷本《雪莱全集》出版，可谓中国雪莱作品译介史的辉煌里程碑。

评论研究
Reviews

"欧洲大诗人"，《新小说》第二卷第二期，1905年。

'Portraits of Great Poets in Europe：Shelley, Goethe and Schiller', *Xin Xiao Shuo* (*New Ficiton*), Vol. 2, No. 2, 1905.

　　1905年，梁启超主编的《新小说》杂志刊登的"欧洲大诗人"肖像中，将雪莱（"英国人斯利"）与席勒（"德国人舍路拉"）、歌德（"德国人哥地"）并列。这是目前所知雪莱的名字第一次进入中国读者的视野。

令飞（鲁迅）《摩罗诗力说》，《河南》杂志第二 / 三号，1908年。

'On the Power of the Satanical School of Poetry' by Ling Fei (Lu Xun), *He Nan*, Nos. 2-3, 1908.

　　1908年，鲁迅在留日学生刊物《河南》发表《摩罗诗力说》，后收入杂文集《坟》。这篇意在"别求新声于异邦"的著名论文将裴伦（拜伦）、修黎（雪莱）作为首先论述的两位诗人，着重强调了他们"立意在反抗，指归在动作"的一面。文中介绍了雪莱的生平与作品，认为他短暂的一生"即无韵之诗"，尤其推崇他"抗伪俗弊习"以及不懈求索自然、人生奥秘的精神。

柳无忌《译苏曼殊潮音序》,《新南社社刊》1924 年第一期。

'Preface to *Chao Yin*' by Su Manshu, trans. by Liu Wuji, *New Nan She Journal*, No. 1, 1924.

仲密（周作人）《诗人席烈的百年忌》,《晨报副刊》1922 年 7 月 18 日。

'The Centenary Commemoration of Shelley's Death' by Zhong Mi (Zhou Zuoren), *Chen Bao Fu Kan*, July 18, 1922.

　　苏曼殊在翻译雪莱、拜伦诗作的同时，也对他们做了比较评论，认为他们虽然"都有创造和恋爱的极高思想"，但拜伦更为偏重行动，雪莱更为偏重思想。此外其诗作《题师梨集》《题拜轮集》和笔记《燕子龛随笔》等作品也对雪莱、拜伦有所评骘。

　　1922 年雪莱逝世百年纪念之际，周作人发表《诗人席烈的百年忌》一文，着重分析雪莱的社会思想，认为他的思想"是建设的，在提示适合理性的想象的社会"，主张非暴力的"无抵抗的反抗主义"。

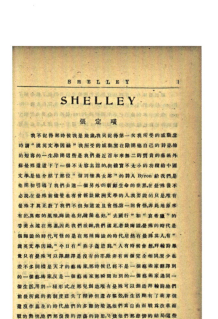
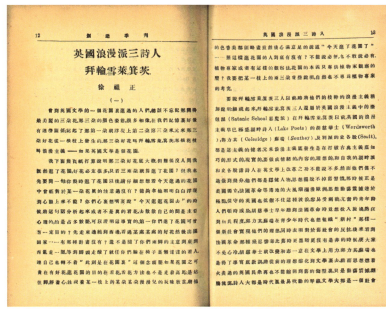

张定璜《Shelley》，徐祖正《英国浪漫派三诗人》，《创造季刊》第一卷第四期，1923 年。
'Shelley' by Zhang Dinghuang; 'Three Poets of the English Romantic School' by Xu Zuzheng, *Chuang Zao Ji Kan* (*Creation Quarterly*), Vol. 1, No. 4, 1923.

　　1923 年，《创造季刊》出版"雪莱纪念栏"，除了刊载《雪莱的诗》《雪莱年谱》之外，还刊登了张定璜、徐祖正的评论文章。张文开头同样将拜伦与雪莱相比较，认为拜伦是"已往的"，雪莱是"我们现在活着的诗人"，着重叙述雪莱的生平事迹。徐文则将拜轮（拜伦）、雪莱、箕茨（济慈）比作英国浪漫主义"那根花枝"上"开得最美丽的三朵花"，着重于这三位诗人的时代背景和艺术特点，认为拜伦"诗中未成品居多"，而雪莱、济慈在艺术上更胜一筹，尤其是雪莱的抒情诗"在英国文学中被称为绝唱"。

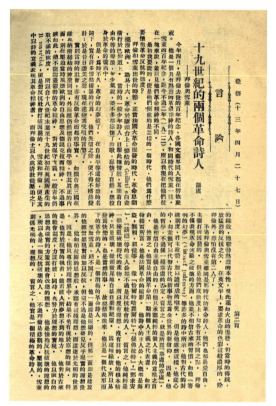

诵虞《十九世纪的两个革命诗人：拜伦与雪莱》,《民国日报》副刊《觉悟》, 1924 年 4 月 27 日。
'Two Revolutionary Poets of the 19th Century：Byron and Shelley' by Song Yu, *Jue Wu*, April 27, 1924.

这一时期还有不少文章将拜伦、雪莱作比较评论，如诵虞《十九世纪的两个革命诗人：拜伦与雪莱》着重分析拜伦、雪莱的革命主张之间的异同，认为拜伦偏向破坏、消极一面，雪莱则偏向建设、积极的一面。

《雪莱生活》，孙席珍编著，世界书局，1929 年。
Life of Shelley by Sun Xizhen, World Book Company, 1929.

《三大诗人的恋爱故事：拜伦、雪莱、歌德》，艾秋编著，美乐图书出版公司，1947 年。
The Love Stories of Three Great Poets：Byron, Shelley and Goethe by Ai Qiu, Mei Le Book Publishing Company, 1947.

　　20 世纪 20 年代至 40 年代，中文世界还出现了不止一种雪莱传记。如孙席珍编著的《雪莱生活》根据几种英美学者的著作，简要叙述了雪莱的生平，并附多幅插图；艾秋《三大诗人的恋爱故事：拜伦、雪莱、歌德》则更偏向故事性、普及性。

[法]莫洛璭《雪莱传》,魏华灼译,商务印书馆,1941年。

Ariel：The Life of Shelley by André Maurois, trans. by Wei Huazhuo, the Commercial Press, 1941.

　　1924年,法国作家、评论家莫洛亚(旧译莫洛璭)的雪莱传记《爱丽儿》出版,在英、美、法等国都畅销一时,影响颇大。莫洛亚在书前小序"致一位好意的读者"中,说明书中所记事件"无疑都是确凿的",引述、立论也都以雪莱著作、书信、友人回忆录等原始资料为依据,但他"竭力把这些真实的素材按事情发展的逻辑整理得井井有条,给人一种自然、清晰的印象,就像小说给人的印象一样"。1941年,魏华灼的中译本由商务印书馆出版。1981年,上海文艺出版社又出版了谭立德、郑其行的译本。

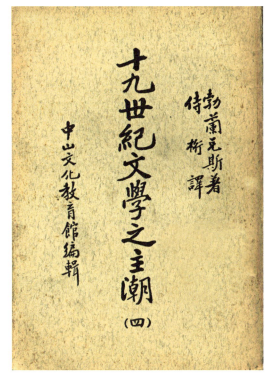

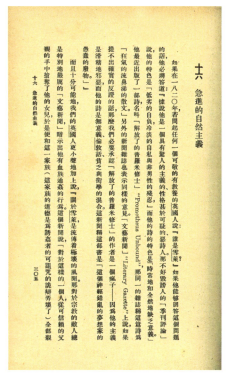

"急进的自然主义"，载［丹］勃兰兑斯《十九世纪文学之主潮》第四册，侍桁译，商务印书馆，1939 年。
'Radical Naturalism', in *Main Currents in Nineteenth Century Literature*, IV by Georg Brandes, trans. by Han Shiheng, the Commercial Press, 1939.

20 世纪 30 年代，著名作家、翻译家韩侍桁（1908 ～ 1987）翻译了丹麦学者、评论家勃兰兑斯（1842 ～ 1927）的文学史名著《十九世纪文学之主潮》。张道真、徐式谷、江枫、张自谋等多位翻译家合译的新译本 1980 年由人民文学出版社出版。其中第四册《英国的自然主义》第十六章《急进的自然主义》专论雪莱，以富于情感的笔法论述了雪莱的生平和创作。

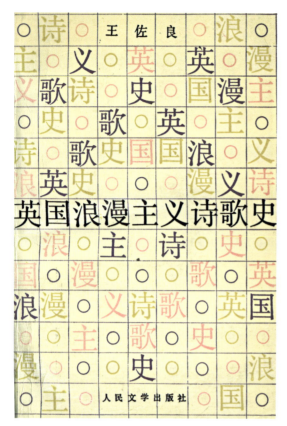

王佐良《英国浪漫主义诗歌史》，人民文学出版社，
1991年。
A History of British Romantic Poetry by Wang
Zuoliang，People's Literature Publishing House，
1991.

　　著名翻译家、学者王佐良在《英国浪漫主义诗歌史》中，认为拜伦虽追求自由，但他的追求"却并不深远"，而雪莱的探索"更带哲学意味，触到更根本的问题"，"人生的苦难感和对于美好社会的追求"在他的作品中"是结合起来的"，详细评述了雪莱的诗歌创作。

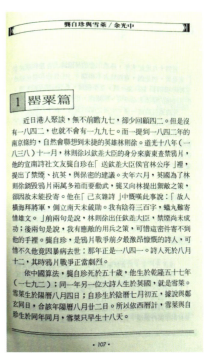

余光中《龚自珍与雪莱》（1984），收入林以亮主编《四海集》，台湾皇冠出版社，1986 年。
'Gong Zizhen and Shelley' by Yu Guangzhong, in *Si Hai Ji*（*A Collection of Critical Essays*）ed. by Lin Yiliang（Song Qi），Crown Publishing House（Taipei），1986.

　　余光中的长篇论文《龚自珍与雪莱》分为《罂粟篇》《声名篇》《童心篇》《侠骨篇》《柔肠篇》五部分，将这两位生于同年同月（公历 1792 年 8 月）的杰出诗人从时代背景、声名起伏、童年情怀、政治意识、情感生活等方面详细比较论述，尤其是大量征引雪莱作品、书信、亲友回忆等原始资料，对雪莱的生平、思想、创作都有独到中肯的论述，堪称中文世界中最杰出的雪莱评论文章之一。

《拜轮诗选》，苏曼殊译，泰东图书局 1923 年四版。
Selected Poems of Byron, trans. by Su Manshu, Tai Dong Book Company, 1923.

"拜伦逝世百年纪念号"，《小说月报》第十五卷 第四期，1924 年。
'The Centenary Commemorative Number of Byron's Death', *The Short Story Magazine*, Vol. 15, No. 4, 1924.

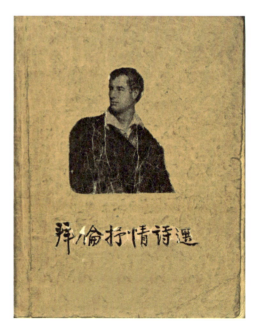

《拜伦抒情诗选》，梁真（查良铮）译， 平明出版社，1955 年。
Selected Lyric Poems of Byron, trans. by Liang Zhen（Zha Liangzheng）, Ping Ming Press, 1955.

《唐璜》，查良铮译，人民文学出版社，1980 年。
Don Juan, trans. by Zha Liangzheng, People's Literature Publishing House, 1980.

《恰尔德·哈洛尔德游记》，杨熙龄译，新文艺出版社，1956 年。
Childe Harold's Pilgrimage, trans. by Yang Xiling, New Literature and Arts Press, 1956.

《拜伦政治讽刺诗选》，邱从乙、邵洵美译，上海译文出版社，1981 年。
Selected Political Ironic Poems of Byron, trans. by Qiu Congyi and Shao Xunmei, Shanghai Translation Publishing House, 1981.

　　拜伦与雪莱生前是志同道合的挚友，而他们在中国也同样广受推崇，而拜伦为支援希腊独立革命而献身的事迹尤其得到钦仰。早在清末，梁启超、马君武、苏曼殊等都翻译过长诗《唐璜》中的著名片断《哀希腊》。此后对拜伦作品的译介几乎从未间断，其中查良铮译《唐璜》等译作早已成为现代中国诗歌翻译的经典之作。此外早在 1924 年拜伦逝世百年之际，《小说月报》就出版了纪念号，可见他在中国声誉之高。

巴金收藏的意大利文《唐·璜》

The Italian version of Byron's *Don Juan*
from the collection of Ba Jin

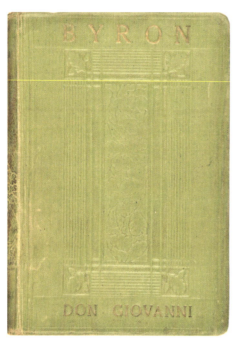
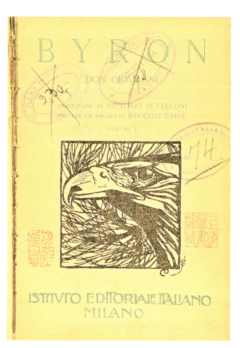

拜伦《唐·璜》(意大利文译本)，维托里奥·贝泰罗尼译，米兰：意大利编辑学院出版社。
Don Giovanni（*Don Juan*）by Lord Byron，Milan：Istituto Editoriale Italiano.

　　作为中国当代最重要的作家、翻译家之一的巴金，广泛收藏世界各国的文学作品。在他捐赠给上海图书馆的外文藏书中，有一套印刷精美的意大利文《唐·璜》。这套图书原藏于上海的一个意大利文化机构 "意大利之家"（Casa d'Italia）。

珀西·比希·雪莱：革命的歌者

吴泽庆

　　珀西·比希·雪莱是英国文学史上重要的浪漫主义诗人之一，也是一位重要的抒情诗人，他的抒情诗强烈奔放、富有原创性。雪莱还是一位散文家、剧作家、翻译家、政论作家。他天性反叛，为工人阶级放歌，人们理所当然地认为他是一位革命浪漫主义诗人。雪莱把他的社会思想和政治思想完美地融入在他的抒情诗中，深深地关注他那个时代的现实。

　　1792 年 8 月 4 日，雪莱出生于英格兰萨塞克斯郡霍舍姆附近菲尔德·普莱斯的一个富裕家庭。年轻时，他因秉持离经叛道的信念而闻名。1802 年，他进入了位于密得塞斯郡勃兰特福德附近的萨昂学院。12 岁时，雪莱被送进伊顿贵族学院，在那里他得到了"疯子雪莱"的绰号；18 岁时，他考入了牛津大学。然而，仅仅六个月后，雪莱因发表《论无神论的必要性》（1811）一文而遭牛津大学开除，这篇文章否定了上帝的存在，父亲也剥夺了他的继承权。同年，雪莱与 16 岁的哈丽艾特·威斯布鲁克私奔。1814 年，雪莱和玛丽·戈德温一起离开英国前往法国。1816 年，哈丽艾特·雪莱自杀后，雪莱和玛丽正式结婚。第二年，这对夫妇离开了英国，定居在意大利。

　　玛丽·雪莱是《弗兰肯斯坦》（1818）的作者，这是世界公认的第一部科幻小说。玛丽的父亲是激进的政治哲学家威廉·戈德温，母亲是哲学家和女权主义者玛丽·沃斯通克拉夫特。雪莱也受到其他一些进步思想家的影响，如利·亨特和托马斯·洛夫·皮科克。1822 年 7 月 8 日，雪莱因乘船在勒里奇附近的斯佩齐亚湾沉没而离世。

　　政治上，雪莱是一个革命者，也是一个民主者，他的矛头直指社会生活中无所不在的残酷、不公正、权威、宗教、暴政和剥削。他的诗歌揭示多种主题：反抗暴政、追求自由和理想的社会秩序、同情被压迫者和提倡打破种种机构禁锢。这些主题散见于他的诗篇之中，如《麦布女王》（1813），《伊斯兰的起义》（1818）、《致英格兰人之歌》（1819）和

《解放了的普罗米修斯》(1820)。同时，雪莱的政治和社会观点影响了英国和欧洲的社会主义运动。同时，革命虽然失败，他对革命的态度反映出他的革命乐观主义精神。

文学上，雪莱是英国最优秀的抒情诗人之一。雪莱的抒情诗富有神话、象征、神话典故、人格化、隐喻和其他修辞手法。正如《西风颂》所表现的，雪莱用他的明快的诗句，表达了强烈的艺术力量；正是借助语言，雪莱充分激发其想象力来理解真理的理想秩序。他的诗时而欢快丰富，充满着色彩、气味、声音、图像，以及韵律美和音乐美，时而纯洁和浓缩。他的诗句中有很多描述大自然的词语：火、空气、水、风和地球等。

雪莱的作品还包括《赞智力之美》(1816)、《勃朗峰》(1816)、《奥兹曼迪亚斯》(1818)、五幕悲剧《钦契》(1819)、《暴政的假面游行》(1819)、《西风颂》(1820)、《云雀》(1820)、挽歌《阿童尼》(1821)以及散文《诗辩》(1821)等。

《西风颂》可以看作雪莱的标志性诗歌，是雪莱最受欢迎和最著名的抒情诗之一。在主题上，这首诗体现了雪莱坚忍的战斗精神和恒久不变的反抗决心；在技巧上，这首诗体现了雪莱诗歌中独特的抒情美。《西风颂》和《解放的普罗米修斯》皆于1820年面世，均为英国浪漫主义运动的力作。

《西风颂》是诗人在1819年秋天的一个傍晚在佛罗伦萨附近的一个树林里构思而成的。"颂歌"是为重大仪式写作的长篇诗歌，形式华美，语气严肃、庄重。诗中将"West Wind"(西风)两个单词大写是对大自然的抽象特点进行拟人化描写，从而赋予其神性或神一样的品质。这首诗包含五个诗节，每节十四行。雪莱在该诗中将十四行诗与意大利三行诗节，即三韵体，结合起来，形成自己独特的诗节，这是一种比较特别的十四行诗，韵式异常复杂，即：五个十四行的五步抑扬格诗节，每节含四个三韵体和结尾的一组两行对偶句，格律为五步抑扬格，韵式为 aba bcb cdc ded ee。这种韵式使读者联想到风变得狂暴起来，把树叶纷纷吹落在地，乌云表明猛烈的暴风雨马上来袭，海面上亦是惊涛骇浪、波涛翻滚。

全诗分为两部分。第一部分包括前三节。每一节中分别描述了西风在地球、天空和海洋肆虐。最后两节则集中描写西风与诗人的关系。其中，第一节重点阐述了西风既是破坏者又是保护者的双重角色，点明了诗的主题。西风是一种破坏力量，因为西风吹掉了仅存的树叶，暴风雨的乌云遮挡了天空；但是，西风又是一种建设性的力量，因为它促进了季节的轮换。诗人由此看到了革命的道理，即革命可以从其失败中汲取力量。生命周期、再生、死亡与生命的联系、结束和开始的盘根错节，这些主题贯穿了全诗。在诗人的想象中，西风的自由不仅在于其自由驰骋，也在于其自由创造与毁坏。尽管冬天会很快到来，但是诗人却备受鼓舞，因为春天和再生也会随着冬天来临。大自然中的再生的力量不仅带来了新的生命，也给诗人带了创作的灵感。

《解放了的普罗米修斯》是一部四幕抒情剧，也是雪莱成就最大的代表作。这个主题来自埃斯库罗斯的悲剧《被缚的普罗米修斯》。剧中，普罗米修斯从天堂偷走了火，被宙斯惩罚，锁在高加索悬崖上，并遭受秃鹫叼食肝脏，痛苦不堪，最终，普罗米修斯与暴君宙斯和解。雪莱的《解放了的普罗米修斯》的情节与希腊悲剧的情节基本一致，但与这个作品的结局有所不同：在普罗米修斯的母亲大地和新娘阿西亚的大力支持下，在冥王和赫拉克勒斯的帮助下，宙斯被逐下王位，普罗米修斯获得了解放。雪莱要为人类创造一个美好世界的愿景，显示了他的革命乐观主义精神。普罗米修斯不屈不挠，是一个理想化的革命者，他蔑视权威，与暴政作斗争。这部戏剧赞扬了人类的潜力，雪莱自己也承认这是他的最完美的作品。对雪莱来说，博爱是治愈人类弊病的良药。作品中的对抗与仇恨被雪莱戏剧中的爱的音符所取代。雪莱在作品中采用了各种各样的抒情诗形式，包括他自己的抒情诗模式和他对一些诗体形式的巧妙改编，如"品达体诗""斯宾塞诗节"和"双行体"等。

《奥兹曼迪亚斯》是一首十四行诗，用松散的五步抑扬格写成，与其他英语十四行诗相比，具有非典型性的韵律格式（ababa cdcedefef），而且没有八行诗和六行诗来划分的结构特征。

作为一首政治诗，《奥兹曼迪亚斯》讲述了拉美西斯二世法老（古希腊人称他为奥兹曼迪亚斯）的故事。他统治埃及66年。这位生活在公元前13世纪的拉美西斯二世雕像的一大块碎片激发了雪莱在1817创作这首诗的热情。奥兹曼迪亚斯傲慢狂妄，盲目自信，自认是王中之王，深陷权力之中。在这首诗中，雪莱表达了一切都将成为历史，消失在时间的海洋之中，包括最伟大的人和他们的帝国。

在《奥兹曼迪亚斯》中，雪莱探讨了帝国统治者衰落的命运，这样的命运不可避免，揭示他们的伟大缺乏真实，具有虚伪性。这首诗的主题多样。首先，这首诗讽刺了权贵。拥有绝对权力的国王仍然无法逃脱最后的争斗，他的国家无法避免迅速毁灭的命运，雪莱嘲笑当权者。其次，探讨了奥兹曼迪亚斯雕塑所象征的艺术与美是瞬间即逝的。奥兹曼迪亚斯的雕塑一直暴露在风雨之下，最后必将破碎不堪、没了生息。时间强大无比，可以摧毁一切。任何完美的事物都不可能永远存在。第三，这首诗反映了时间是永恒的。权力、艺术和美都随着时间的流逝而消失。强大的时间摧毁一切，包括成功、幸福和辉煌。人的命运无法改变，时间无法超越。

雪莱也是一位政治作家。这座雕像象征着过去的力量，最终，人类会无能为力。在《奥兹曼迪亚斯》中，雪莱洞察权力、名声和政治遗产问题。他认为政治领导是短暂的，会被遗忘，统治者没有能力保留自己的伟大。在雪莱看来，名望和权力都是虚幻的。

吴泽庆

中央民族大学外国语学院教授，北京外国语大学文学博士。中国外国文学学会英国文学分会常务理事、中国外国文学学会英语文学分会理事。英国剑桥大学、美国德克萨斯大学访问学者。主要研究领域为英美文学。

Percy Bysshe Shelly: Revolutionary Voice

Wu Zeqing

Percy Bysshe Shelly is one of the most famous English Romantic poets and his lyric poems display spontaneity and originality. He was also an essayist, dramatist, translator, and pamphleteer. Being a rebel by nature and a voice for the working class, Shelley is justifiably considered to be a poet of revolutionary romanticism in England. He responded to current events by integrating his social and political thoughts into lyrical verse.

Shelly was born into a wealthy family on August 4 1792, in Field Place near Horsham, Sussex, England. He was known for his nonconformist beliefs from a young age. In 1802, he attended Syon House Academy in Brentford, Middlesex. When he was 12, Shelley entered Eton College, where he got the nickname 'Mad Shelly'. At the age of 18, he entered Oxford University, only to be expelled six months later for a pamphlet titled *The Necessity of Atheism* (1811), which repudiated the existence of God. He was then disinherited by his father. In the same year, Shelley eloped with 16-year-old Harriet Westbrook. In 1814, Shelley left England for France with Mary Godwin. After Harriet Westbrook committed suicide in 1816, Shelley and Mary officially married. In the following year, the couple left England and settled in Italy.

Mary Shelley was the author of *Frankenstein* (1818), often considered to be the first universally acknowledged science fiction novel. Her father was the radical political philosopher William Godwin, and her mother was the philosopher and feminist Mary Wollstonecraft. Not only was Percy Bysshe Shelley influenced by the ideas of his wife and her parents, he also responded to other progressive thinkers such as Leigh Hunt and Thomas Love Peacock. On July 8, 1822, Shelley drowned while sailing in the Bay of Spezia, near Lerici.

Politically, Shelley was a revolutionary and a democrat, and he attacked cruelty, injustice, authority, religion, tyranny, and oppression prevalent in society at the time. Themes including the protest against tyranny, the quest for freedom, promotion of an ideal social order, sympathy for the oppressed and an advocation for the destruction of various established institutions reoccur in poems such as *Queen Mab* (1813), *Song To The Men Of England* (1819), *Revolt of Islam* (1818), and *Prometheus Unbound* (1820). Shelley's political and social views profoundly influenced social movements that sought change in England and Europe. Moreover, his attitude towards the fall of the French monarchy during the French Revolution reflected the anti-establishmentarianism that had begun to emerge in Britain at this time.

Shelley's verses are rich in myth, symbolism, allusions, personification, metaphors and other rhetorics. As demonstrated in 'Ode to the West Wind', Shelley uses the lucidity of his lines to convey strong dramatic power. The poetic language, which reflects his wild imagination, clearly depicts the perfect order of truth. His poetry is often rich, joyous and full of colour, flavour, sound and image. His rhymes and music contain themes of purity and austerity. His verses are filled with terms describing the elements of nature: fire, air, water, wind, and earth.

Shelley's works also include *Hymn to Intellectual Beauty* (1816), *Mont Blanc* (1816), *Ozymandias* (1818), *The Cenci. A Tragedy, in Five Acts* (1819), *The Mask of Anarchy* (1819), *Ode to the West Wind* (1820), *To a Sky-Lark* (1820), *Adonais* (1821) and *A Defence of Poetry* (1821).

'Ode to the West Wind' is often seen as Shelley's signature poem and is one of the most popular and well-known of his lyric verses. Thematically, the poem demonstrates Shelley's tenacious fighting spirit and uncompromising rebellious nature. Technically, the poem is endowed with his extraordinary lyrical beauty. 'Ode to the West Wind' was published with *Prometheus Unbound* in 1820, another masterpiece of the English Romantic movement. The inspiration for 'Ode to the West Wind' came during a visit to a wood near Florence on an autumn evening in 1819. Odes are elaborately formal lyric poems often taking the form of a lengthy ceremonial address to a person or abstract entity. They are always serious and elevated in tone. The capitalization of the words 'West' and 'Wind' in the poem was made to personify an abstract quality or aspect of nature and to endow it with a divine or god-like quality. The poem contains five stanzas of 14 lines each. Shelley created his own stanza, a variant of the original Italian pattern which fused elements of the sonnet with those of the Italian three-line rhyme scheme known as terza rima: five 14-lined stanzas of iambic pentameter, with each stanza containing four tercets and a closing couplet. The metrical pattern is iambic pentameter and the rhyme scheme is aba, bcb, cdc, ded, ee. This scheme allows readers to picture how the wind became furious, tearing leaves off trees while the clouds imply a impending storm with waves running high.

The poem is divided into two parts. The first part contains the first three stanzas which each describe the power of the West Wind over the earth, the sky and the sea, respectively. The last two stanzas focus on the relation between the West Wind and the poet. The first stanza focuses on the double role of the West Wind as both destroyer and preserver which is also the main theme of the poem. The West Wind is a destructive force because it drives off the remaining leaves and clouds in the sky, but it is also a positive force because it contributes to the cycle of the seasons. The poem is seen to contain Revolutionary references in that nature's regeneration, like revolution, often gets its initial momentum from destruction. Themes of the cycle of life, regeneration, and the interconnectedness of life and death, endings and beginnings, run throughout 'Ode to the West Wind'. The wind can not go anywhere it pleases, but it has the freedom to create and destroy. Although winter will soon arrive, the poetical voice in 'Ode to the West Wind' is greatly encouraged, for spring and regeneration will follow the winter. The regenerative powers of Nature will not only bring new life, but also bring poetic creation.

Prometheus Unbound, a four-act lyrical drama, is considered Shelley's greatest achievement. The subject is drawn from *Prometheus Bound*, a classic tragedy attributed to Aeschylus, in which Prometheus, who had stolen the fire from Heaven, was punished by Zeus by being chained to the Caucasian Cliff with vultures feeding on his liver. In this story Prometheus finally reconciled with the tyrant Zeus. The plot of Shelley's *Prometheus Unbound* echoes that of the Greek tragedy, but differs from its classic counterpart in the ending. With the strong support of Earth, Prometheus' mother, Asia, his bride, and additional help from Demogorgon and Hercules, Zeus is driven from the throne and Prometheus is emancipated. The vision of a better world for mankind shows Shelley's revolutionary optimism. Prometheus is idealized as a revolutionary with an unyielding spirit, which defies authority and fights tyranny. The drama praises man's potential, and Shelley himself acknowledged it as 'the most perfect of my products'. To Shelley, universal love was the cure for the ills of human life. Confrontation and hate is replaced by notes of love in Shelley's drama. He employed various lyric forms in this piece, including his own lyric patterns and those he dexterously adapted, such as the Pindaric ode, the Spenserian stanza, and couplets.

'Ozymandias' is a sonnet written in loose iambic pentameter. Compared to other sonnets written in the English language, 'Ozymandias' contains an atypical rhyme scheme (ababa cdcedefef) without the octave-and-sestet structure.

'Ozymandias' is a political poem which tells a story about pharaoh Ramesses II who ruled Egypt for 66 years. A large fragment of a statue of Ramesses II from the 13th century BCE inspired Shelley to write the poem in 1817. Ozymandias was arrogant, overconfident and obsessed with power. He regarded himself as the king of kings. In the poem, Shelley suggested that everything, including great men and their empires, would become a part of history and be lost in the sea of time.

In 'Ozymandias', Shelley explored the inevitable decline of leaders of empires and their pretensions to greatness. The theme of this poem covers many aspects. Firstly, this poem satirizes the powerful. The king with absolute power still cannot escape struggles, and his country has no way of avoiding its rapid destruction. Shelley mocked people in power. Secondly, this poem suggests that art and beauty, which the sculpture of Ozymandias symbolizes, is momentary and fleeting. The sculpture of Ozymandias was exposed to continual rain and wind and untimately destroyed, demonstrating the power of time. No perfect thing would exist forever. Thirdly, this poem suggests the permanence of time. Power, art and beauty disappear as time passes by. Powerful time destroys everything including success, happiness and brilliance. A human being's fate is determined and the passing of time is impossible to halt.

Shelley was also a political writer. The statue of Ozymandias symbolizes power and strength of the past, which man is ultimately powerless over . In 'Ozymandias', Shelly highlighted aspects of power, fame, and political legacy, suggesting that political leadership is fleeting and will be forgotten, and a ruler is unable to preserve his greatness. In Shelly's view, fame and power were mere illusions.

Wu Zeqing

Professor of English, School of Foreign Studies in Minzu University of China, whose research interest is British and American literature. He earned his Ph.D. in Literature at the Beijing Foreign Studies University. He is an Executive Director of British Literature Branch of Chinese Foreign Literature Society, and a member of English Literature Branch of Chinese Foreign Literature Association. He was a visiting scholar at Cambridge University and the University of Texas, U.S.A.

thereto!"

Then he stretched his hand out to be led: I took the
hand, held it a moment to my lips, then let it pass round my
shoulder; being so much lower of stature than he, I served
both for his prop and guide. We entered the wood and
wended homeward.

Conclusion.

Reader — I married him. A quiet wedding we had:
the parson and clerk were alone present. When we got
from church, I went into the kitchen of the Manor-house,
Mary was cooking the dinner, and John, cleaning the knives,
said:

Mary — I have been married to Mr Rochester this morn-
he housekeeper and her husband were both of that decent
—matic order of people, to whom one may at any time sa-
communicate a remarkable piece of news without incurr-
—anger of having one's ears pierced by some shrill ejaculat-
—ubsequently stunned by a torrent of wordy wonderment
—did look up, and she did stare at me, the ladle with
—he was basting a pair of chickens roasting at the fire, did
—ome three minutes hang suspended in air, and for

II

夏洛蒂·勃朗特

CHARLOTTE
BRONTË

Portrait of Charlotte Brontë engraved by J.C. Armytage after George Richmond, published by Smith, Elder & Co, London, 1857, from 'A collection of engraved and lithographed portraits of English poetesses made by F.J. Stainforth' , British Library 1876.f.22.

夏洛蒂·勃朗特肖像，J.C. 阿米蒂奇仿照乔治·里士满的画作所刻，由史密斯与埃尔德出版公司出版，伦敦，1857 年，选自《F.J. 斯坦福思所作英国女诗人肖像版画集》。大英图书馆藏 : 1876.f.22.

夏洛蒂·勃朗特是19世纪英国著名作家，1816年4月21日出生于英国北部约克郡。父亲帕特里克·勃朗特和母亲玛利亚·勃兰威尔婚后共育有子女六人，夏洛蒂有两个姐姐、一个弟弟、两个妹妹。因父亲任约克郡哈沃斯教区牧师，夏洛蒂四岁时举家迁至哈沃斯生活，次年母亲就去世了。1824年，两个姐姐和夏洛蒂先后进入柯文桥一所寄宿制学校就读，一年后姐姐们染病相继辞世。1827年，刚过十岁的夏洛蒂与弟妹开始创作实践。1831年，夏洛蒂进入罗海德的伍勒女子学校学习，一年多后离开。1835年，她回到该学校任教师，两个妹妹随后进入这所学校学习。1839年，夏洛蒂开始任家庭教师。1842年，夏洛蒂和妹妹艾米莉前往布鲁塞尔的埃热夫妇创办的学校就读，1844年返回家中，自办学校未果。1846年，夏洛蒂和两个妹妹，艾米莉·勃朗特（Emily Brontë）和安妮·勃朗特（Anne Brontë），分别以男性化的笔名柯勒（Currer Bell）、艾力斯（Ellis Bell）和艾克顿·贝尔（Acton Bell）合著出版了诗集。同年，夏洛蒂完成了小说处女作《教师》(*The Professor*)，但屡遭出版社退稿，说是内容平淡。然而，她并不气馁，随后开始创作《简·爱》(*Jane Eyre*)，1847年以笔名柯勒·贝尔出版。引起当时社会的巨大反响后，随即两次再版。1848年至1849年，夏洛蒂的弟弟和两个妹妹相继去世。夏洛蒂继续坚持创作，于1849年出版了第二部小说《雪莉》(*Shelly*)，1853年出版了第三部小说《维莱特》(*Villette*)。1854年6月，夏洛蒂与父亲的副牧师尼克尔结婚，1855年3月31日，夏洛蒂英年早逝。1857年，尼克尔联系出版了她的作品《教师》。1947年，伦敦威斯敏斯特教堂（或译西敏寺）的"诗人角"中为夏洛蒂·勃朗特树立了纪念牌，标志着对夏洛蒂的纪念上升到国家级别。

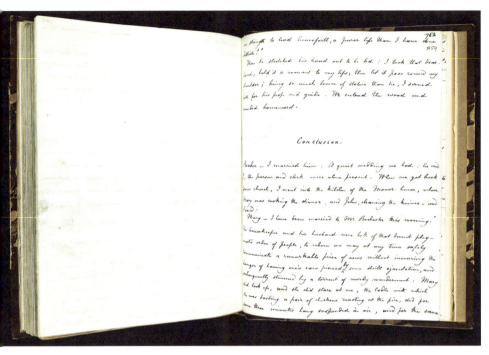

Manuscript fair copy of *Jane Eyre*, volume III by Charlotte Brontë, 1847, open at folio 259r. British Library Add MS 43476.

《简·爱》创作手稿誊写本，第三卷，夏洛蒂·勃朗特作，1847 年，打开页为第 259 页。大英图书馆藏：Add MS 43476.

Charlotte Brontë (1816–55) is best known for her semi-autobiographical novel, *Jane Eyre* which was published in 1847 under the male pseudonym 'Currer Bell'. The novel tells the story of Jane Eyre, a governess who falls in love with her employer, Edward Rochester. Yet Rochester is hiding a dark secret, in the form of his mentally ill wife, who is locked away in the attic. The story encompasses themes of love, marriage, mystery and terror, often set against a romantic landscape.

夏洛蒂·勃朗特（1816 ～ 1855）最有名的作品是她的半自传体小说《简·爱》。1847 年，此书以男性笔名柯勒·贝尔首次出版。小说讲述了家庭女教师简·爱深深地爱上了雇主爱德华·罗切斯特的故事。然而罗切斯特却隐藏着一个黑暗的秘密——庄园的阁楼里锁着他那精神失常的妻子。故事涵盖了爱、婚姻、神秘和恐怖的主题，故事背景大多设定在富有浪漫主义气息的英国田园中。

The British Library holds the original neat or 'fair' copy manuscript of *Jane Eyre* which was sent to the publishers Smith, Elder & Co. The manuscript was originally written as one volume with the folios being consecutively numbered throughout although it is now bound in three volumes. **[Fig. 1]** The manuscript is a copy in Brontë's hand, of an earlier draft as some errors in transcription can be seen, for example in volume III on folios 2, 113 and 254. Although this manuscript was a final and neat version, Brontë has made corrections to the text, demonstrating that the story remained a work in progress even at a late stage. The manuscript had been rejected by a number of publishers but in August 1847 it was sent to George Smith of Smith, Elder & Co, who said of his first encounter with the manuscript 'After breakfast on Sunday morning I took the manuscript of *Jane Eyre* to the library and began to read it. The story quickly took me captive … before I went to bed that night I had finished the manuscript. My literary judgment was perfectly satisfied'. The novel appeared in print just two months later.

大英图书馆收藏了《简·爱》字迹工整的原稿，即校正版誊写稿。当年，勃朗特正是将这份手稿交予史密斯与埃尔德出版公司。作者最初将手稿整理为一整卷，每页均标有页码，而今天我们看到的这份手稿分三卷装订（图1）。这份手稿是勃朗特根据一份更早的创作手稿亲笔誊写而成，上面还可以看到一些抄写时出错的地方，如第三卷第2页、第113页和第254页。虽然这份最终版手稿十分整洁，但勃朗特还是对文本有所修改，也就是说即使是在最后阶段，作者仍然对故事进行不断的修改和创作。最初，很多出版商都拒绝出版这部作品。1847年8月，史密斯与埃尔德出版公司的出版商乔治·史密斯收到了这份手稿。在提起第一次读到这部作品时，史密斯这样说道："周日早上吃完早饭，我拿起《简·爱》的手稿到书房开始读。这个故事马上吸引了我，当天晚上睡觉前我就读完了，这部小说完全满足了我对文学的期许。"仅仅两个月后，作品付梓。

Fig.1

©British Library Board

Manuscript fair copy of *Jane Eyre,* volume III by Charlotte Brontë, 1847, British Library Add MS 43476.

《简·爱》创作手稿誊写本，第三卷，夏洛蒂·勃朗特作，1847年。大英图书馆藏：Add MS 43476.

Not only was this the manuscript sent to George Smith, it was also used by the printers. Compositors or typsetters worked from the manuscript, selecting letters called 'type' and setting them onto a tray called a 'forme' held together by a frame or 'chase' from which to print pages of the novel. The manuscript bears the names of different typesetters working with the text as well as inky fingerprints across some pages. [Fig. 2]

这份乔治·史密斯读过的手稿也是印刷时使用的版本。排字工人根据手稿先挑出需要使用的"活字",将它们放在被称为"印版"的托盘上,然后用叫做"版框"的边框固定好,接下来就可以将小说一页一页地印出来了。这份手稿上还有当时负责印刷的几位工人的名字,一些页面上还能看到沾了油墨的指印。(图2)

Fig.2

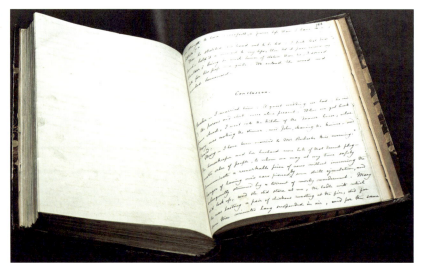

©British Library Board

Image showing fingerprints and type compositor's name in pencil on manuscript fair copy of *Jane Eyre*, volume III by Charlotte Brontë, 1847, British Library Add MS 43476, f 259r.

手稿上有很多排字工人沾了油墨的指印,还有几位工人的铅笔签名。《简·爱》创作手稿誊写本,第三卷,夏洛蒂·勃朗特作,1847年。大英图书馆藏:Add MS 43476,f 259r.

Fig.3

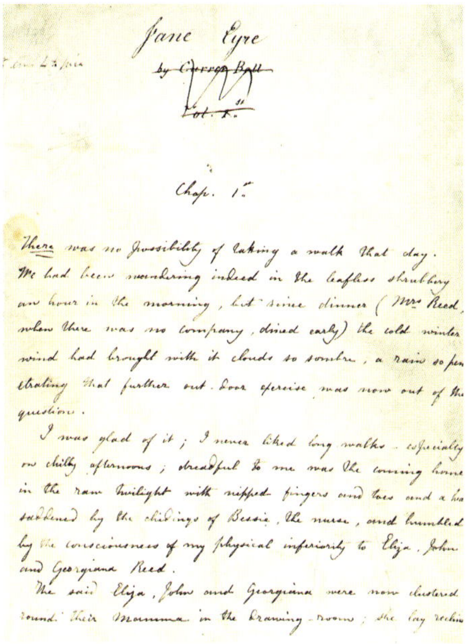

Jane Eyre
~~by Currer Bell~~
~~Vol. I.~~

Chap. 1st

There was no possibility of taking a walk that day. We had been wandering indeed in the leafless shrubbery an hour in the morning, but since dinner (Mrs Reed, when there was no company, dined early) the cold winter wind had brought with it clouds so sombre, a rain so penetrating that further out-door exercise was now out of the question.

I was glad of it; I never liked long walks - especially on chilly afternoons; dreadful to me was the coming home in the raw twilight with nipped fingers and toes and a heart saddened by the chidings of Bessie, the nurse, and humbled by the consciousness of my physical inferiority to Eliza, John and Georgiana Reed.

The said Eliza, John and Georgiana were now clustered round their mamma in the drawing-room; she lay reclin

Title page of manuscript fair copy of *Jane Eyre*, volume I by Charlotte Brontë, 1847, British Library Add MS 43476, f 1r.

《简·爱》创作手稿誊写本的第一卷扉页，夏洛蒂·勃朗特作，1847 年。大英图书馆藏：Add MS 43476，f 1r.

The title page in volume I shows the name 'Currer Bell' which has been crossed out. **[Fig. 3]** Brontë felt the male name would give her novels more credibility, as well as preventing her acquaintances from identifying the real people and places in her writing. The third volume contains the conclusion of the novel with the famous line 'Reader, I married him' which refers to the marriage between Jane Eyre and Mr Rochester. **[Fig. 4]**

手稿的第一卷的扉页上写有“柯勒·贝尔”这个名字，但是被划掉了（图 3）。因为勃朗特觉得使用男性笔名会让她的小说更容易被接受，同时也可以防止认识她的人将她笔下的人物和故事发生的地点与现实对号入座。第三卷结尾点出故事结局的是那句经典的“读者，我嫁给了他”，这句话表明简·爱与罗切斯特先生终成眷属。（图 4）

Fig.4

262
259

me strength to lead henceforth, a purer life than I have done hitherto!"

Then he stretched his hand out to be led: I took that dear hand, held it a moment to my lips, then let it pass round my shoulder; being so much lower of stature than he, I served both for his prop and guide. We entered the wood and wended homeward.

Conclusion.

Reader – I married him. A quiet wedding we had: he and I, the parson and clerk were alone present. When we got back from church, I went into the kitchen of the Manor-house, where Mary was cooking the dinner, and John, cleaning the knives – and I said:

Mary – I have been married to Mr Rochester this morning." The housekeeper and her husband were both of that decent phlegmatic order of people, to whom one may at any time safely communicate a remarkable piece of news without incurring the danger of having one's ears pierced by some shrill ejaculation, and subsequently stunned by a torrent of wordy wonderment. Mary did look up, and she did stare at me, the ladle with which she was basting a pair of chickens roasting at the fire, did for some three minutes hang suspended in air, and for the same

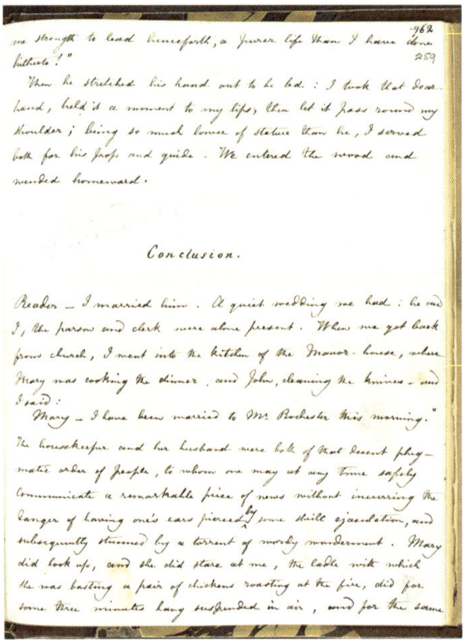

Conclusion of manuscript fair copy of *Jane Eyre*, volume III by Charlotte Brontë, 1847, British Library Add MS 43476, f 259r.

《简·爱》的结尾，《简·爱》创作手稿誊写本，第三卷，夏洛蒂·勃朗特作，1847 年。大英图书馆藏：Add MS 43476，f 259r.

This manuscript has a provenance which can be traced directly back to the original publisher of *Jane Eyre*, George Smith. It was bequeathed to the British Museum Library (now the British Library), by Mrs Elizabeth Smith, (subject to a life-interest of her children) as a memorial of her late husband, George Murray Smith, the son of George Smith. In 1933 the three surviving children decided to relinquish their further life-interest in the manuscript and transferred them to the British Museum Library.

这份手稿的来源可以直接追溯到小说最早的出版商乔治·史密斯。伊丽莎白·史密斯女士将手稿作为遗赠交与当时的大英博物馆图书馆，也就是今天的大英图书馆，以纪念她已逝的丈夫、乔治·史密斯的儿子——乔治·默里·史密斯。不过她的孩子们依旧拥有手稿的终身财产所有权。1933 年，她的三位后代决定放弃手稿的终身所有权，将其移交给大英博物馆图书馆。

夏洛蒂·勃朗特作品在中国
Charlotte Brontë's works in China

夏洛蒂·勃朗特发表的小说数量虽不多，但其思想内涵和艺术成就已超过了同时代的许多作家。《简·爱》是夏洛蒂的代表作，它也是最早在中国被译介的勃朗特姐妹的作品。百余年来，《简·爱》翻译者众多，优秀的翻译作品也非常突出，常常一再重版，成为翻译史上佳话。《简·爱》的译本形式也多种多样，有缩译本、节译本、全译本、改写本、双语对照本等。在不同历史时期，中国人对《简·爱》评介的侧重点和态度也大相径庭。20世纪二三十年代，它被当作言情小说和爱情故事进行翻译和介绍，对原文有较多删减和修改；1949年后，译文逐渐完整并忠实原著；改革开放以来，随着外国文学作品出版的繁荣，对勃朗特姐妹作品的译介和研究达到了高潮，尤其是《简·爱》的翻译和研究论文具有相当的数量。20世纪八九十年代，国内掀起了阅读和研究勃朗特姐妹作品的新高潮，出现了电影、话剧等多种艺术改编形式。为满足读者的阅读需求，盖斯凯尔夫人（Elizabeth Cleghorn Gaskell）的重要传记作品《夏洛蒂·勃朗特传》也在1987年翻译出版。《简·爱》至今仍活跃在世界舞台上，保持着艺术活力。

作品译介
Translations

《简·爱》在中国的翻译历程
Translations of *Jane Eyre* in China

《重光记》(《简·爱》故事节略本)，周瘦鹃译，收入
《心弦》，大东书局，1925 年。
Chong Guang Ji (*Jane Eyre*), an abridged
version trans. by Zhou Shoujuan, published in the
book *Xin Xian*, Da Dong Publishing House, 1925.

　　据现有的资料，夏洛蒂作品最早的汉译可能是周瘦鹃的《简·爱》故事节略本《重光记》，收录于 1925 年 7 月上海大东书局出版的《心弦》中。《心弦》是言情丛书 "我们的情侣" 之第四册，是周瘦鹃或缩译或摘编的西方爱情小说集。周瘦鹃认为《简·爱》"尤其算得一部极伟大的言情小说"，并认为它带有自传色彩。周瘦鹃对作品本身的定位和理解存在局限性，翻译的风格也具有明显的鸳鸯蝴蝶派特点。

《孤女飘零记》，伍光建节译本，商务印书馆，1935 年。
Gu Nü Piao Ling Ji (*Jane Eyre*), a partial version trans. by Wu Guangjian, the Commercial Press, 1935.

　　在 1930 年代，我国出现了两个《简·爱》的中译本，分别是伍光建的节译本《孤女飘零记》（商务印书馆，1935）和李霁野的全译本《简爱自传》（上海生活书店，1936）。《孤女飘零记》是商务印书馆"万有文库"中的一种。伍光建重视《简·爱》创作的独特性，认为"此作不依傍前人，独出心裁，描写女子性情，其写女子之爱情，尤为深透，非男著作家所可及"。他从人物品格方面高度评价《简·爱》，称其"于描写女子爱情之中，同时并写其富贵不能淫，贫贱不能移，威武不能屈气概，为女子立最高人格"，是 20 世纪二三十年代中翻译家对作品理解的一大进步。

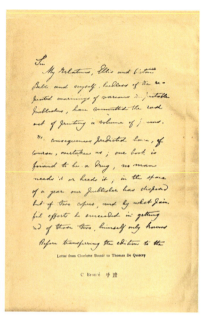

《简爱自传》，李霁野译，上海生活书店，1936 年。
Autobiography of Jane Eyre，a complete version trans. by Li Jiye, Shanghai Life Publishing House，1936.

　　《简爱自传》于 1936 年 9 月由上海生活书店初版，收入郑振铎主编"世界文库"丛书，是一部根据原著再版翻译的全译本。此译本中收录了作者的再版序。这篇重要序言使我国读者了解到当时某些权势阶层对《简·爱》的责难和诋毁及作者的反击。

　　李霁野（1904～1997），我国著名作家、翻译家。1922 年开始发表作品，有散文集、杂文集、专著和译著近二十种。与韦素园、台静农、韦丛芜等成立"未名社"。曾在鲁迅的指导下从事翻译、写作、出版等工作。1949 年以后曾任南开大学外文系教授、天津市文化局局长、天津市文联主席等职。

李霁野《简爱自传》后以《简爱》之名多次再版，包括上海文化生活出版社（1946 年沪一版，1949 年沪四版）、上海新文艺出版社（1956）、上海文艺出版社（1962）、陕西人民出版社（1982）等。

Jane Eyre is also published by Shanghai Culture Life Publishing House（1946, 1949）, New Literature & Art Publishing House（1956）, Shanghai Literature & Art Publishing House（1962）and Shaanxi People's Publishing House（1982）trans. by Li Jiye.

《简·爱》，祝庆英译，上海译文出版社，1980 年。
Jane Eyre, a complete version trans. by Zhu Qingying, Shanghai Translation Publishing House，1980.

　　20 世纪 80 年代初，上海译文出版社出版了祝庆英译《简·爱》，这是至今国内流传最广的译本之一。祝庆英评价《简·爱》为"英国文学史上一部有显著地位的小说，成为世界闻名的一部小说，是因为它成功地塑造了一个敢于反抗、敢于争取自由和平等地位的妇女形象"，"反映了妇女摆脱男子的压迫和歧视的要求，在英国文学史上是一个创举，难怪它的出现在当时的社会上引起了那样强烈的反响"。值得注意的是，祝庆英在肯定《简·爱》的艺术成就之余，对它的结局并未持赞赏态度，表达了个性鲜明的观点："简·爱苦尽甘来，有情人终成眷属，读者心理上可能多少得到一点儿安慰，但是全书的现实主义的力量却削弱了。这个结尾不能不说是蛇足。"

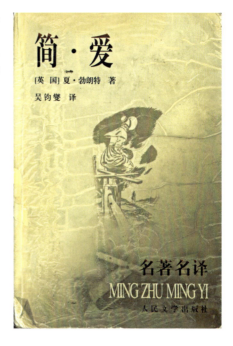

《简・爱》，吴钧燮译，人民文学出版社，
1990 年。
Jane Eyre, a complete version trans.
by Wu Junxie, People's Literature
Publishing House, 1990.

　　20 世纪八九十年代，外国文学作品的阅读和研究日益繁荣，吴钧燮译《简・爱》由人民
文学出版社于 1990 年初版，是传读甚广的译本。他认为这部作品自诞生起一百多年来，之所
以能获得如此巨大的成功，是因为"对生活的真切体验是一切好作品的最根本条件之一"，并
认为"它创作了英国文学（而且不只是英国文学）中第一个对爱情、生活、社会以至宗教都采
取了独立自主、积极进取态度的女性形象，是读者从来不曾遇见过的"。同时，吴钧燮也看到
了作者的局限性，并指出在《简・爱》的整个情节中多少带有当时流行的"哥特式小说"的神
秘气氛。

《简·爱》，黄源深译，译林出版社，1994 年，上海图书馆中国文化名人手稿馆藏签名本。
Jane Eyre, a complete version trans. by Huang Yuanshen, Yilin Press, 1994. (This book is collected by the China Cultural Celebrities Manuscript Library of Shanghai Library with the translator's signature on the cover page.)

  1994 年，黄源深译《简·爱》由译林出版社初版，后来多次再版和重印，深受读者欢迎。上海图书馆中国文化名人手稿馆藏有此书典藏版的译者签名本，由黄源深签赠于 2002 年 12 月。

  黄源深认为简·爱身上所表现出的追求自由、平等和维护人的尊严的信念和举动，其实反映了工业革命后新兴的资产阶级的要求。他认为作者的思想倾向"非常明确，对旧价值观的攻击十分犀利"。在肯定了《简·爱》的艺术成就之外，也指出了它的不足之处："书中过多的巧合不但有媚俗之嫌，而且也易导致小说失真"，"男女主人公之间情感的表达过于夸张，不免显得有些矫情"。但"《简·爱》毕竟还是读者所喜爱的《简·爱》"。

《简爱》"夏绿蒂·勃朗特诞生 200 周年纪念特别版"
Jane Eyre, Charlotte Brontë's 200th anniversary
special edition, 2016.

　　英国文学在港台地区的译介也非常兴盛，1935 年香港南国出版社的《红豆》杂志就专门印行了一期"英国文坛十杰专号"，详细介绍了十位英国作家。台湾也有多家出版社出版了别具特色的译本，如《简爱》附珍藏书签的译本（2017），《简爱》"夏绿蒂·勃朗特诞生 200 周年纪念特别版"译本（2016），《简爱》改写本英语读本（2015），《简爱》原创漫画本（2014）《简爱》新译本（2013）等。

《简·爱》译名举隅 (The Chinese names for *Jane Eyre* and Jane Eyre)

书　名	译　者	作者译名	主角译名
《重光记》（1925）	周瘦鹃	嘉绿白朗蝶	嫣痕伊尔
《孤女飘零记》（1935）	伍光建	夏罗德·布纶忒	柆晤·爱迩
《简爱自传》（1936）	李霁野	C. 白朗底	简·爱
《简·爱》（1980）	祝庆英	夏洛蒂·勃朗特	简·爱
《简·爱》（1990）	吴钧燮	夏·勃朗特	简·爱
《简·爱》（1994）	黄源深	夏洛蒂·勃朗特	简·爱
《简爱》（2016）	张玄竺	夏绿蒂·勃朗特	简爱

夏洛蒂·勃朗特其他作品在中国的译介情况
Other translations of Charlotte Brontë's works

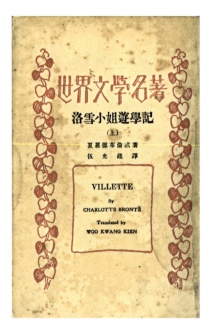

《洛雪小姐游学记》，伍光建译，商务印书馆，1926 年。
Luo Xue Xiao Jie You Xue Ji (*Villette*), trans. by Wu Guangjian,
the Commercial Press, 1926.

　　除《简·爱》外，夏洛蒂的作品 *Villette* 也深受中国读者喜爱，汉译本有 1926 年商务印书馆出版的伍光建译《洛雪小姐游学记》。译者在序中认为《孤女飘零记》（即《简·爱》）和《洛雪小姐游学记》"齐名，或谓后作胜过前作"，"其描写爱情，不若前作之如火如荼，而更为深刻"，高度评价这部作品"为近日小说家开风气之先耳"。

《维莱特》，吴钧陶、西海译，上海译文出版社，1994 年。
Villette, trans. by Wu Juntao, Xi Hai, Shanghai Translation Publishing House, 1994.

　　吴钧陶是我国著名翻译家，屠岸先生评价他为"在苦难中熬过来的诗人兼翻译家"。吴钧陶、西海译《维莱特》是近年具有代表性的译本，于 1994 年由上海译文出版社出版。湖南文艺出版社在 1987 年出版了谢素台译《维莱特》，也是较为知名的译本。

评论研究
Reviews

林德育《泰西女小说家论略》,《妇女杂志》
第三卷第十二期, 1917 年。
'The story of female novelists of western
countries' by Lin Deyu, *Women Magazine*,
Vol. 3, No. 12, 1917.

国内早期提到勃朗特姐妹的文章,是刊于《妇女杂志》第三卷第十二期"记述门"中的《泰西女小说家论略》,该文署名"闽侯林德育女士"。文中列举了"欧美女小说家十人,共为十大端",认为她们"皆足以激进女学界,自强自立之志者也",勃朗特姐妹名列其中,被誉为"三凤齐飞",作者认为三人"皆以小说诗词名,而沙洛德尤著"。

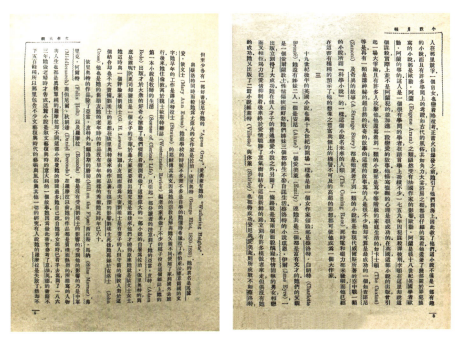

郑振铎《文学大纲》第二十八章《十九世纪的英国小说》,《小说月报》第十七卷第六期，1926 年。
'Outline of Literature：English novels of the 19th century' by Zheng Zhenduo, *The Short Story Magazine*, Vol. 17, No. 6，1926.

　　1926 年，我国著名学者、翻译家郑振铎（1898 ～ 1958）在《文学大纲》第二十八章"十九世纪的英国小说"（刊于《小说月报》第十七卷第六期）中向中国读者介绍了勃朗特姐妹的创作，并评价《简·爱》为"在佳人才子的普通恋爱小说之外，另辟了一条路，就是写两个面貌丑寝、性情固执的男女，相恋而又相拒，竭力把爱情抑制着，后来终于爱情战胜了意气而相结合。这个新鲜的路，立刻有许多模仿者来走，但俱没有她的成功"。

郑次川《欧美近代小说史》，商务印书馆，1927 年。
Modern History of European and American Novels by Zheng Cichuan, the Commercial Press, 1927.

金石声《欧洲文学史纲》，神州国光社，1931 年。
The Outline of the History of European Literature by Jin Shisheng, Shen Zhou Guo Guang Publishing House, 1931.

20 世纪二三十年代，出现了多部介绍欧美文学作品的著作，郑次川和金石声曾在自己的著作《欧美近代小说史》（商务印书馆，1927）和《欧洲文学史纲》（神州国光社，1931）中对夏洛蒂和她的作品进行了评介。郑次川把夏洛蒂·勃朗特划归在"写实主义时代"的作家中，对她给予了很高的评价："女小说家第一可数的，是夏罗德布纶忒。"金石声认为夏洛蒂的作品"都是成功的作品"，但是他把《简·爱》仅看作"恋爱小说"，有其时代的局限性。

仲华《英国文学史中的白朗脱氏姊妹》,《妇女杂志》第十七卷第七期"妇女与文学专号",1931 年。
'The Brontë sisters in the history of English literature' by Zhong Hua, *Women Magazine*, Vol. 17, No. 7 'Special issue on women and literature', 1931.

　　《妇女杂志》在 1931 年第十七卷第七期"妇女与文学专号"上刊有"白朗脱氏三姊妹"的肖像,并发表了仲华的文章《英国文学史中的白朗脱氏姊妹》。经过五四新文化运动的洗礼,旧观念及旧陋习逐渐被时代淘汰,妇女解放的话题日益受到关注。仲华不仅对勃朗特姐妹的生平作了详细介绍,还绘声绘色地叙述了《简·爱》的诞生过程。他指出"在英国文学史上杰出的女作家中,白朗脱氏姊妹是很值得我们注意的",认为她们的作品"是攻读文学者所必备的书"。

金东雷《英国文学史纲》，商务印书馆，1937 年。
The Outline of the History of English Literature by Jin Donglei, the Commercial Press, 1937.

　　金东雷著《英国文学史纲》于 1937 年 2 月由商务印书馆出版，由蔡元培和蒋梦麟先生分别题写书名。书中介绍了勃朗特姐妹的文学创作并大加赞赏。吴康撰写的序言值得一读，他在当时就认识到中英两国文学交流对于文化合作的深远意义，并发出阅读的倡议："尤其是英国人，应当买来读读，可以使他们明了，研究英国人内心生活及文学价值的学者，中国是大有人在！这个说法，对中英文化合作的前途，不见得没有关系罢？"可以说是相当有远见的观点，也体现了文化自信。

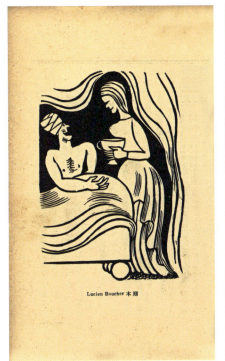

茅盾《〈真亚耳〉的两个译本》,《译文》1937 年新二卷第五期。
'Two Chinese translations of Jane Eyre' by Mao Dun (Shen Yanbing), *The Translation Magazine*,
New Vol. 2, No. 5, 1937.

　　1937 年，茅盾在《译文》杂志上发表《〈真亚耳〉的两个译本》，对伍光建和李霁野的译本做了评论："我们需要西洋名著的节译本（如伍先生的工作），以飨一般的读者，但是也需要完善的全译本直译本，以备'文艺学徒'的研究"，"《真亚耳》虽不是怎样了不起的杰作，可是居然有那么两种好译本，实是可喜的事"。表现了当时的历史背景下，知识分子对文学作品关注的层面和对国外作品在中国译介的一种看法。

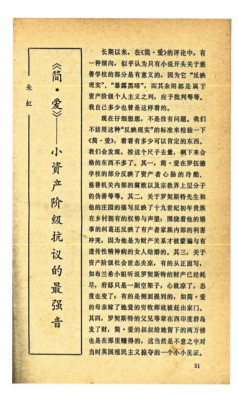

朱虹《〈简·爱〉——小资产阶级抗议的最强音》，《读书》1979 年第 5 期。

'*Jane Eyre*：The strongest protest of the petty bourgeoisie' by Zhu Hong, *Du Shu*, No. 5, 1979.

王化学《说〈简·爱〉》，《外国文学研究》1980 年第 2 期。

'Studies on Jane Eyre' by Wang Huaxue, *Foreign Literature Research*, No. 2, 1980.

李霁野《夏洛特·勃朗蒂和她的创作》，《外国文学研究》
1980 年第 3 期。
'Charlotte Brontë and her masterpieces' by Li Jiye,
Foreign Literature Research, No. 3, 1980.

　　改革开放初期，我国掀起了外国文学的翻译、评论和阅读的高潮。就夏洛蒂的作品
而言，各种文学评论层出不穷，研究文章多达七十篇左右，具代表性的有老一辈翻译家李
霁野的《夏洛蒂·勃朗特和她的创作》(《外国文学研究》1980 年第 3 期)、研究专家朱虹
的《〈简·爱〉——小资产阶级抗议的最强音》(《读书》，1979 年第 5 期)、王化学的《说
〈简·爱〉》(《外国文学研究》，1980 年第 2 期) 等。

杨静远《夏洛蒂·勃朗特小说中的爱情主题》,《文学评论》1980 年第 5 期。

'The love theme in Charlotte Brontë's novels' by Yang Jingyuan, *Literature Review*, No. 5, 1980.

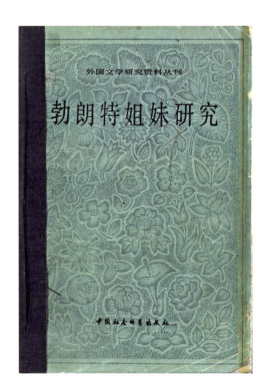

杨静远编选《勃朗特姐妹研究》,中国社会科学出版社,
1983 年。

The Research on the Brontë Sisters, selected and edited by Yang Jingyuan, China Social Sciences Press, 1983.

杨静远《勃朗特姐妹的生平及其创作》,《名作欣赏》
1986 年第 3 期。
'The life and masterpieces of the Brontë Sisters'
by Yang Jingyuan, *Masterpiece Appreciation*,
No. 3, 1986.

勃朗特姐妹的生平及其创作

杨静远

五、普通读者心目中的勃朗特姐妹

　　杨静远（1923～　　）是我国著名翻译家、外国文学研究专家。1983 年，她编选了《勃朗特姐妹研究》，由中国科学出版社出版。这是一部较为全面地汇集了勃朗特姐妹自述、评论和生平资料的研究文集。

　　杨静远在其《勃朗特姐妹的生平及其创作》一文中提到，1955 年夏洛蒂逝世一百周年时，威斯敏斯特教堂内举行了一个纪念仪式，献词中高度评价了夏洛蒂的成就："夏洛蒂曾被誉为最强有力的浪漫主义作家和第一位现实主义作家；她把想象、激情和经验触（融）为一体，就这点来说，没有人能超越她"，"夏洛蒂成名快，但任何作家都不能由他的同代人盖棺论定。必须经过五十年、一百年，经过背景、审美观、鉴赏标准和研究方法各异的几代人，批评家和公众，才能对他作出合理的结论。夏洛蒂必须等待二十世纪对她做出最后的裁决。到这时候，她终于在一致公认下取得了不朽的地位"。杨静远认为这样的论断是"朴实、清醒、公正的"。

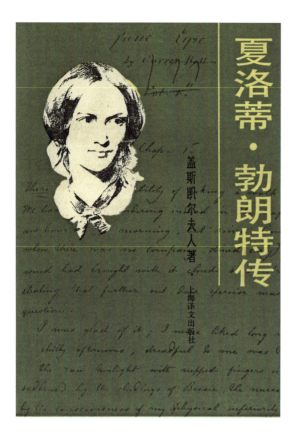

[英] 盖斯凯尔《夏洛蒂·勃朗特传》，祝庆英、祝文光译，上海译文出版社，1987 年。
The Life of Charlotte Brontë, by Elizabeth Cleghorn Gaskell, trans. by Zhu Qingying & Zhu Wenguang, Shanghai Translation Publishing House, 1987.

夏洛蒂·勃朗特过世后，盖斯凯尔夫人（Elizabeth Cleghorn Gaskell）受老勃朗特先生委托，于 1857 年为夏洛蒂撰写出版了传记。这是人们了解夏洛蒂生平与创作的重要材料。一百多年后，祝庆英、祝文光将之译介给了中国读者。祝庆英认为："一位著名的女作家为同时代的另一位女作家写传，写出一部真实生动、至今仍激动人心的传记，这在文学史上也许是极少见的事。"

戴锦华、滕威《〈简·爱〉的光影转世》，上海人民出版社，2014年。
Research on Jane Eyre Movies by Dai Jinhua, Teng Wei, Shanghai People's Publishing House, 2014.

冯茜《英国的石楠花在中国：勃朗特姐妹作品在中国的流布及影响》，中国社会科学出版社，2008年。
The British Heather in China：The Spread and Influence of Brontë's works in China by Feng Qian, China Social Sciences Press，2008.

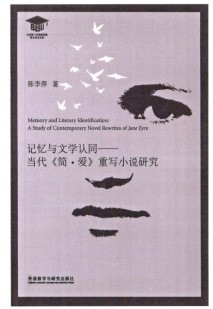

陈李萍《记忆与文学认同：当代〈简·爱〉重写小说研究》，外语教学与研究出版社，2015年。
Memory and Literary Identification：A Study of Contemporary Novel Rewrites of Jane Eyre by Chen-Li Ping，Foreign Language Teaching and Research Press，2015.

[美] 吉尔伯特、古芭《阁楼上的疯女人：女性作家与 19 世纪文学想象》，杨莉馨译，上海人民出版社，2015 年。
The Mad Women In the Attic, by Sandra M. Gilbert, Susan Gubar, trans. by Yang Lixin, Shanghai People's Publishing House, 2015.

　　进入 21 世纪以来，外国文学研究在我国呈现出日新月异的面貌，研究思路更为广阔，角度更加新颖。对夏洛蒂·勃朗特及其作品的研究中，较为优秀的著作有《英国的石楠花在中国：勃朗特姐妹作品在中国的流布及影响》《〈简·爱〉的光影转世》《记忆与文学认同：当代〈简·爱〉重写小说研究》，还有译著《阁楼上的疯女人：女性作家与 19 世纪文学想象》，等等。

"青苔石边的紫罗兰"：有故事的夏洛蒂·勃朗特

王　欣

19 世纪维多利亚时期的英国，小说已经代替诗歌成为最主要的文学形式。这段时期人们受教育水平提高，出版业蓬勃发展，读者群开始增加，促进了小说的创作。"据估计，维多利亚女王统治时期，出版了 42000 多本小说，尤以 19 世纪中期的出版最为集中。"[1] 从文学史的角度而言，19 世纪中期的小说创作堪称"维多利亚的正午时光"[2]，出现了狄更斯、勃朗特姐妹、萨克雷等一批杰出作家。

勃朗特姐妹是英国文学史中一道亮丽的风景，夏洛蒂、艾米莉和安妮三姐妹写出了各具特色的小说，同时也反映出家庭共性的特征："激情""压抑""冷静现实主义与哥特式幻想的奇妙结合"等。[3] 对于三人的文学创作，夏洛蒂说是自己偶然间发现了妹妹艾米莉写的诗，并开始鼓励她发表自己的作品。或许是出于自己女性的身份焦虑，或许是对文学创作的不够自信，姐妹三人于 1846 年用贝尔家族三兄弟之名（柯勒、艾力斯、艾克顿）一起合作出版了一部《诗集》(Poems by Currer, Ellis, and Acton Bell)，贝尔兄弟即是勃朗特姐妹。尽管这部诗集只售出两本，但将这三姐妹们正式引上了文学创作之路，并最终留给了世界读者宝贵的《简·爱》《呼啸山庄》以及《女房客》等经典名作。

夏洛蒂是帕特里克·勃朗特夫妇的三女儿，其父亲出生于爱尔兰，早年通过自己的努力来到英国，就读于剑桥大学圣约翰学院，随后在约克郡任牧师。勃朗特的母亲玛利亚·布兰威尔出生于潘赞斯（Penzance），家境殷实。夏洛蒂于 1816 年 4 月 21 日出生于父亲任职的桑顿教区，4 岁时随家人搬到了哈沃斯（Haworth）小镇。在哈沃斯，勃朗特

1　Sean Purchase, *Key Concepts in Victorian Literature*, Shanghai：Shanghai Foreign Language Education Press, 2016, p. 170.

2　Sean Purchase, Op. Cit., p. 168.

3　Margaret Homans, 'The Brontës' in Kastan, David Scott, ed., *The Oxford Encyclopedia of British Literature*, Vol. 1, Shanghai：Shanghai Foreign Language Education Press, 2009, p. 275.

先生忙于教堂事务和照顾病弱的勃朗特夫人，再加上性格的孤僻与固执，一家人基本上过着离群索居的生活，对于孩子们来讲尤为如此，她们只能在想象的世界中实现与人交往、沟通的愿望。相对封闭的家庭生活，反而赋予了孩子们更多想象的空间。他们一起阅读，一起游戏，也一起创作。当父亲给了孩子们一箱木质玩偶士兵时，她们便有了发挥丰富想象力的媒介。这些士兵有了名字，开始在各种故事中扮演角色，而这些故事大多是由夏洛蒂编撰出来的。

夏洛蒂是个瘦小、沉静、看起来有些古板的女孩。母亲早逝，两个姐姐相继夭折，这样的家境迫使她早早成熟起来。对于一个内心孤独、渴望温暖的孩子来说，文学阅读与文学创作开启了一片自由又轻松的天空，为其保留了一份细腻、丰富的情感追求。在盖斯凯尔夫人为夏洛蒂所写的传记中，她提到了自己所收藏的一份宝贵的手稿："这主要是夏洛蒂撰写的故事、戏剧、诗歌及传奇，不用放大镜几乎不可能看清上面写了什么。……我复印了一份她手稿中的作品目录，足以说明她当时对文学有着怎样的热爱。"[1] 这个目录夏洛蒂完成于 1830 年 8 月 3 日，列举了自己写于 1829 年至 1830 年间的作品，包括《爱尔兰历险记》(The Adventures in Ireland) 等传奇故事、话剧《打油诗人》(The Poetaster) 以及两本诗歌集，当时她只有 14 岁。

在夏洛蒂写给好友的一封信中，她列了一个长长的书单，推荐给朋友阅读，更重要的是这份书单中夹杂着夏洛蒂自己对于那些文学作品的评价，表现出一个成熟的读者才有的智慧与批判。"你如果喜欢诗歌，那就读第一流的诗歌，比如弥尔顿、莎士比亚、汤姆逊（Thomson）、戈德史密斯（Goldsmith）、蒲柏（尽管我并不喜欢他，但你倒可以一读）、司各特、拜伦、坎贝尔（Campbell）、华兹华斯和骚塞等人的作品。不要对莎士比亚和拜伦这两个名字感到惊叹，他们两位文如其人，都很伟大。这样你就会知道如何选择优秀的而避开糟糕的；最美的篇章常常是最纯净的，而糟糕的作品则令人生厌，你绝不会有再次阅读的欲望。莎士比亚的喜剧以及拜伦的《唐璜》和《该隐》都可忽略不读，尽管拜伦的《唐璜》是首恢弘壮丽的诗歌……"[2]

夏洛蒂共创作了四部小说，其中第一部《教师》并未获得出版商的青睐，第二部《简·爱》则在 1847 年出版后大获成功。《简·爱》是一本自传性小说，第一版的封面

---

1 Elizabeth Gaskell, *The Life of Charlotte Brontë,* Middlesex: Penguin Books, 1975, p. 112.
2 Elizabeth Gaskell, Op. Cit., p. 151.

上明确标注有"自传"的字样，在人物塑造、情景设计、故事情节等多方面展现出作者童年的印迹。勃朗特姐妹年幼时都曾就读过的位于考恩桥的牧师学校，通常被认为是《简·爱》中洛伍德（Lowood）寄宿学校的原型。卡恩桥学校管理不善，孩子们的校餐特别差，这样艰苦的条件也是夏洛蒂两个姐姐幼年夭折的主要原因，而夏洛蒂则在小说创作中对姐姐的遭遇表达了同情与愤慨，姐姐的形象即是小说中死于肺病的好友海伦（Helen Burns）。

《简·爱》以现实主义的笔触，描写了受压制的女家庭教师简·爱如何通过婚姻的方式来获得最后的幸福，是一部"温热的、愤怒的、受委屈的、大声疾呼式的、振奋的"作品。[1] 一百余年来，简·爱与罗切斯特的爱情故事感动了无数读者，小说中"你以为我穷、卑微、相貌平凡、身材矮小，我就没有灵魂、没有心吗？你想错了！"等经典对白常为人所引用，小说的艺术手法与精神品质更是吸引了众多文评家的研究兴趣，常读常新。《简·爱》作为一部经典的成长小说，体现出个人对于生活中各种不幸的积极对抗，从压迫到自由，从被动到主动，实现了个人的成长与成熟。这种个人主义的、代表了正在成长中的资产阶级的思想也正反映出英国维多利亚文学的核心特征，个人命运的改变、社会地位与经济地位的提升，既是个人性格使然，也是具有一定偶然性特点的外在因素的结果，这种特征在后来狄更斯的《远大前程》等现实主义小说中都是一脉相承的。

夏洛蒂的另外两部小说是《雪莉》（*Shirley*）和《维莱特》（*Villette*），分别发表于 1849 年和 1853 年。两部作品中也或多或少融入了作者个人生活的痕迹，比如夏洛蒂 15 岁时（1831 年 1 月）就读的距离哈沃斯不足 20 英里的罗黑德学校（Roe Head），以及学校附近的奥克威尔礼堂（Oakwell Hall），都被写入了另一部小说《雪莉》中。在罗黑德学校期间，夏洛蒂获得了老师和同学们的尊敬和喜爱；也是在这里，她结交了两位非常要好的朋友艾伦·纽西和玛丽·泰勒。与两位挚友之间的大量通信，成为理解夏洛蒂及其作品的重要文献。

夏洛蒂的故事点点滴滴汇聚到了她的作品中，她仿若华兹华斯笔下的那朵"青苔石边的紫罗兰"，远离繁花，静吐芬芳。夏洛蒂尽管作品不多，却留给了我们非常丰富的文

1　Heather Glen, *The Cambridge Companion to the Brontës*, Shanghai: Shanghai Foreign Language Education Press, 2004, p. 99.

学遗产，她的家乡哈沃斯已经成为文学圣地，受到来自世界各地文学爱好者的"朝拜"，对她最经典的作品《简·爱》也有着诸多的电影等其他艺术形式的改编，更有当代作家对它的改写。对于夏洛蒂作品的研究，也在不断丰富着当代女性主义文学批评等理论视角，不断带给读者和研究者更多更新的收获，这恐怕就是夏洛蒂的魅力所在吧。

王　欣

上海外国语大学英语学院教授，博士生导师。上海市外国文学学会理事、副秘书长，中国外国文学学会比较文学与跨文化研究会理事。主要从事英美文学、比较文学方向的研究。

'A Violet by a Mossy Stone': the Life of Charlotte Brontë

Wang Xin

In the Victorian age, novels took the place of poetry as the most popular literary form. The Victorian period saw the improvement of education, as well as the prosperity of the publishing industry. As a result, there was an increased reading public, which accordingly encouraged novel writing. 'It has been estimated that during Victoria's reign (1837–1901) over 42, 000 novels were published, and the mid-century year between 1847 and 1851 were especially prolific'.[1] In terms of literary history, novel writing in the mid-Victorian period is generally considered to be the 'Victorian Noon-Time', for there appeared such great novelists as Dickens, the Brontë sisters, and William Makepeace Thackeray.[2]

The Brontë sisters are usually described collectively in the history of British literature, and they produced works with distinctive and often shared characteristics: 'passion', 'repression', and 'startling combinations of hardheaded realism and gothic fantasy'.[3] Remarking on the literary career of herself and her sisters, Charlotte said she once happened to find poetry written by Emily and then encouraged her to have it published. It was either out of anxiety about their female identity or due to the lack of confidence in their writing that, in 1846, the sisters had their first collection of poems published under the pseudonyms of Currer, Ellis, and Acton Bell. In spite of the fact that the collection sold only two copies, it set them on the path to pursue literature as a formal career, which brought about the classic works *Jane Eyre*, *Wuthering Heights*, and *The Tenant of Wildfell Hall*.

Charlotte was the third daughter of the family. Her father Patrick Brontë was born in Ireland and went to study at St John's College, Cambridge, working later in Yorkshire as a curate. Her

---

1 Sean Purchase Cit., *Key Concepts in Victorian Literature*, Shanghai: Shanghai Foreign Language Education Press, 2016, p. 170.
2 Sean Purchase, Op. Cit., p. 168.
3 Margaret Homans. 'The Brontës'. in Kastan, David Scott, ed., *The Oxford Encyclopedia of British Literature*, Vol. 1, Shanghai: Shanghai Foreign Language Education Press, 2009, p. 275.

mother Maria Branwell was born into a fairly well-off family in Penzance. Charlotte was born in Thornton on April 21 1861, and at four years old moved to Haworth with her family. The fact that Mr Brontë was somewhat unsociable and obstinate, and usually busy with his church duties and taking care of his sick wife, lead to a solitary life for the family. The children could only satisfy their needs for social communication in an imaginary world. They read together, played together, and wrote together. A box of wooden soldiers given by Mr Brontë to his son Branwell became the means for the children to give full play to their imagination. They named those soldiers and endowed them with life by having them play different roles in their own stories, the most part of which were made up by Charlotte.

Charlotte was small, silent and seemed a little conservative. The death of her mother and her two elder sisters was devastating, and she was obliged to mature at an early age. For a child yearning for care and understanding, reading and writing might be a desirable means to relieve the burden and pursue the ideal. In the biography *The Life of Charlotte Brontë*, Elizabeth Gaskell mentioned an exquisite manuscript in her possession, in which there was a list of works written by Charlotte: '...tales, dramas, poems, romances, written principally by Charlotte, in a hand which it is almost impossible to decipher without the aid of a magnifying glass ...Among these papers there is a list of her works, which I copy, as a curious proof how early the rage for literary composition had seized upon her'.[1] The list was made on August 3, 1830, when Charlotte was only 14 years old, recording works she wrote between 1829 and 1830, such as *The Adventures in Ireland*, *The Poetaster*, and collections of poetry.

In a letter to her friend, Charlotte made a long list of recommended readings. What is more impressive is that the list was mixed with her critical comment on those works, which shows the wisdom and judgment characteristic of a mature reader. 'If you like poetry, let it be first-rate; Milton, Shakespeare, Thomson, Goldsmith, Pope (if you will, though I don't admire him), Scott, Byron, Campbell, Wordsworth, and Southey. Now don't be startled at the names of Shakespeare and Byron. Both these were great men, and their works are like themselves. You will know how to choose the good, and to avoid the evil; the finest passages are always the purest, the bad are invariably revolting; you will never wish to read them over twice. Omit the comedies of Shakespeare and the *Don Juan*, perhaps the *Cain*, of Byron, though the latter is a magnificent

---

1   Elizabeth Gaskell, *The Life of Charlotte Brontë*, Middlesex: Penguin Books, 1975, p. 112.

poem ... '.[1]

Charlotte produced four novels, the first of which, *The Professor*, was not favorably received by publishers. It was eventually published posthumously in 1857. However, her second book *Jane Eyre,* proved to be a great success. Considered to be a semi-autobiographical story, it contains many traces of its author's childhood experiences, in terms of characterization, setting, and plot. The Cowan's Bridge school the Brontë sisters had attended is usually regarded as the prototype of Lowood Boarding School in *Jane Eyre*. The school located at Cowan's Bridge was not well managed, and the food there was awful. The harsh conditions more or less caused the death of Charlotte's two elder sisters. Charlotte conveyed her compassion for her sisters and indignation at their treatment in *Jane Eyre* through the character of Helen Burns.

Jane Eyre depicts in a realistic style how the repressed governess achieved her happy ending via marriage, and it is a story that is 'hot: angry, aggrieved, clamorous, exhilarated'.[2] Since its publication, *Jane Eyre* has moved countless readers by the love story between Jane and Rochester. Dialogues such as, 'Do you think, because I am poor, obscure, plain, and little, I am soulless and heartless? You think wrong!', have been repeatedly quoted over time. Besides, the techniques and themes of the novel have attracted the attention of many critics, who have kept coming up with new findings.

Jane Eyre as a typical Bildungsroman, shows the individual's positive fight against a myriad of adversities in life. It depicts how the individual achieved growth and maturity, from bondage to freedom and, from passiveness to activity. The individualism as the ideology of the growing bourgeoisie is one of the key features of Victorian novels. The ability to change one's fate, as well as elevating of one's social and economic status, is depicted as the result of both the individual character and the contingent external elements. Such a feature is also embodied in Dickens's works like *Great Expectations*.

The other two novels by Charlotte Brontë are *Shirley* and *Villette*, which were respectively published in 1849 and 1853. In the two books, traces of Charlotte's own life experience could be found. Take *Shirley* as an example whereby the school in Roe Head attended by Charlotte from 1831, which was less than 20 miles from Haworth where Charlotte lived, and the Oakwell Hall in the vicinity of the school, were both written into *Shirley*. During her time at the school, Charlotte

---

1　Elizabeth Gaskell, Op. Cit., p. 151.
2　Heather Glen, *The Cambridge Companion to the Brontës*, Shanghai: Shanghai Foreign Language Education Press, 2004, p. 99.

won respect from both teachers and classmates, and it was here that she made friends with two girls, Ellen Nussey and Mary Tyler. The letters between these friends have been important sources for understanding Charlotte and her works.

Charlotte's experiences were often written, into her works. She is like 'a violet by a mossy stone' depicted in Wordsworth's 'She Dwelt among the Untrodden Ways', quiet, secluded, but fragrant. Though Charlotte was not that prolific at novel writing, she does leave us a generous literary legacy. Her hometown of Haworth has become a well known literary sanctuary, welcoming millions of tourists from all parts of the world. There have been a large number of adaptations of *Jane Eyre*, on screen and in other art forms, and in addition, the contemporary rewriting of the story also takes shape in different ways. The study of Charlotte's works paved the way for the development of modern literary theories like feminism, thus providing additional and newer perspectives for readers and researchers. This is the charm and grace of Charlotte Brontë.

Wang Xin

Professor of English in the School of English Studies at Shanghai International Studies University, Council Member of the Association of Comparative Literature and Transcultural Studies and Shanghai Foreign Literature Association. Teaches and researches in British Romanticism, Victorian literature, the English Poetic Tradition, and Modern Poetry.

47

ual as clockwork."

"So he is," said Mr Pickwick, brighten
ood boy, that. I'll give him a shill
ly. Now then Sam, wheel away."

"Hold on Sir"— replied Mr Weller with y
the prospect of refreshments "out
young leathers. You walley my f
don't upset me, as the gen'lm'n
driver when they was
n' him to Tyburn." and quicke
pace to a sharp run, Mr Weller
led his master nimbly to the
shot him dexterously out,
side of the basket, and prev
pack it with the utmost dispa
"Weal pie," said Mr Weller solilsqui
arrayed the eatables on the grass.
good thing is a weal pie when yo
the lady as made it, and is su
t aint 'kittens; and arter all thou
the odds, when theyre so like we
the very piemen theirselves, don't
the difference?"

III

查尔斯·狄更斯

CHARLES
DICKENS

Portrait of Charles Dickens at his writing desk from *The Life of Charles Dickens* by John Forster, (London: Chapman & Hall, 1872–74), British Library Dex.316., f 129.

查尔斯·狄更斯在书桌前，图片选自约翰·福斯特著《查尔斯·狄更斯的一生》（伦敦：查普曼与霍尔出版公司，1872～1874年）。大英图书馆藏：Dex.316., f.129.

查尔斯·狄更斯 是 19 世纪英国最伟大的小说家，其作品至今在世界各国流传不衰。他于 1812 年 2 月 7 日生于英国朴茨茅斯，自幼爱好文学与戏剧。1824 年，年仅 12 岁的狄更斯因父亲欠债入狱而被迫辍学数月，到鞋油作坊做工。这段痛苦屈辱的经历给狄更斯留下了终生难以磨灭的印象，也令他对儿童与穷人产生了深切的同情。成年之后，狄更斯从事过律师事务所职员、法院书记员、报社记者等多种工作，积累了丰富的社会阅历。1833 年起，他以"博兹"为笔名，为各家报刊创作小说、随笔数十篇，1836 年结集为《博兹特写集》出版。同年春，《匹克威克外传》（1836～1837）开始连载，短短数月间，书中几位主角的名字在全英国已经家喻户晓。随后的《奥立弗·退斯特》（1837～1839）、《尼古拉斯·尼克尔贝》（1838～1839）、《老古玩店》（1840～1841）等长篇小说同样大获成功，进一步奠定了狄更斯的文坛地位。此后的《董贝父子》（1846～1848）、《大卫·科波菲尔》（1849～1850）、《荒凉山庄》（1852～1853）、《艰难时世》（1854）、《小杜丽》（1855～1857）等小说主题愈加严肃深刻，艺术手法也更为严谨成熟。1856 年，狄更斯买下了自幼向往的肯特郡盖兹山庄，在这里写下了《双城记》（1859）、《远大前程》（1860～1861）、《我们共同的朋友》（1864～1865）等晚期代表作。晚年的狄更斯忙于写作、编辑、巡回朗诵等活动，繁重的工作严重损害了他的健康。1870 年 6 月 9 日，狄更斯在盖兹山庄家中因中风去世，留下了未完成的长篇小说《德鲁德疑案》，身后安葬于威斯敏斯特大教堂"诗人角"。

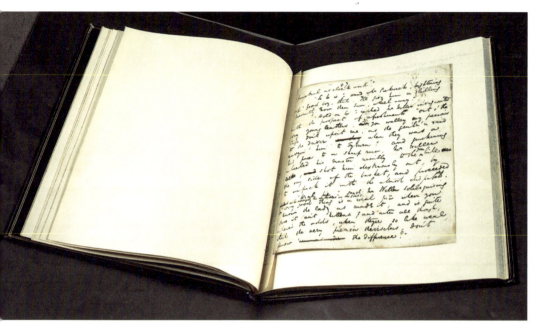

Manuscript for part of chapter 19 of *The Pickwick Papers* by Charles Dickens, 1836–37, British Library Add MS 39182, f 2r.

《匹克威克外传》第 19 章部分手稿，查尔斯·狄更斯著，1836 年至 1837 年。大英图书馆藏：Add MS 39182，f 2r.

The Pickwick Papers is a series of sketches by Charles Dickens (1812–70) about the fictional club founded by Samuel Pickwick, which was intended to be 'A record of perambulations, perils, travels, and adventures'. The stories were published in 19 monthly parts, on sale for one shilling, from 1836 to 1837, and they marked the beginning of Dickens' career as a popular writer. Dickens had been working as a journalist and parliamentary reporter when he was approached by the publishers Chapman and Hall to write text for a series of sporting illustrations

《匹克威克外传》是查尔斯·狄更斯（1812 ～ 1870）创作的系列故事集，故事的主人公是塞缪尔·匹克威克建立的一个虚构团体。这部故事集意在"记录漫游、奇遇、旅行与历险的过程"。从 1836 年至 1837 年，这些故事分 19 期按月出版，每期的售价为一先令。这部小说标志着狄更斯开始成为一位流行作家。在此之前，狄更斯是一名议会报道记者，直到查普曼与霍尔出版公司开始请他为艺术家罗伯特·西蒙的体育插画配上文字。狄更斯并

by the artist Robert Seymour. Yet, rather than simply illustrating the images with text, Dickens set about writing the beginnings of *The Pickwick Papers*. After Seymour tragically died in 1836, Dickens continued the series with illustrations by Robert Buss and Hablot Knight Browne. Each part was issued in a blue wrapper and contained illustrations. [Fig. 1] At the end of the series in 1837, the stories were published as a single novel.

没有把这项工作视作为图配文这么简单的事，而是着手写出了《匹克威克外传》的开篇。西蒙不幸于 1836 年去世，但狄更斯并没有停止这一系列作品的创作，之后的插画由罗伯特·巴斯和赫伯特·奈特·布朗绘制。每一期出版时均有蓝色封皮，并配有插图（图 1）。1837 年该系列完结后，所有故事收录为一整部小说出版发行。

The posthumous papers of the Pickwick Club by 'Boz.' (Charles Dickens), No 1, (London: Chapman & Hall, 1836), original serial with blue wrapper, British Library C.58.f.20.

《匹克威克俱乐部外传》，"博兹"（查尔斯·狄更斯曾用笔名）编著，第一期，（伦敦：查普曼与霍尔出版公司，1836 年），以蓝色封皮装订的原版期刊。大英图书馆藏：C.58.f.20.

Fig.1

The British Library owns two manuscripts for small sections of *The Pickwick Papers*. The larger of the two, Add MS 39182, comprises five folios or leaves and contains the account of the shooting-party luncheon where Mr Pickwick drinks too much punch. **[Fig. 2]** This was published in chapter 19 in the novel and as part 7. The folios are numbered 47–51. Dickens numbered each manuscript installment separately before it was sent to the printers for the monthly publication. The manuscript is written in iron gall ink on wove paper. Iron gall ink is made from tannin (most often taken from oak marble galls produced by the eggs of gall wasps laid on oak trees), vitriol (iron sulphate), gum and water and is extremely acidic. On this manuscript it has begun to eat through the paper in places where Dickens has applied more ink when crossing out words and sentences. Wove paper is a uniform paper made in a fine wire mesh tray which does not have lines or watermarks. This type of paper was widely available in England from about 1780.

大英图书馆藏有《匹克威克外传》故事中一小部分的两份手稿。藏品编号为 Add MS 39182 的是二者中较长的一个，有五张手稿，讲的是在一次狩猎午餐会上，匹克威克先生喝了太多潘趣酒的故事（图 2）。这个故事是小说的第 19 章，按期出版时的第 7 期。手稿页码为第 47 页至第 51 页。在每月将手稿交予印刷厂之前，狄更斯都会单独标出页码。手稿用鞣酸铁墨水在布纹纸上写成，鞣酸铁墨水的成分是单宁酸（通常来自橡木上的瘿蜂卵生出的橡木瘿）、蓝矾（硫酸铁）、树胶和水，因而酸性很强。在这份手稿上，由于狄更斯涂抹圈划的一些地方用墨较多，墨水已经开始渗透纸张。布纹纸规格统一，在细丝网盘中制成，没有横纹也没有水印。约 1780 年起，这种纸在英国被广泛使用。

Fig.2

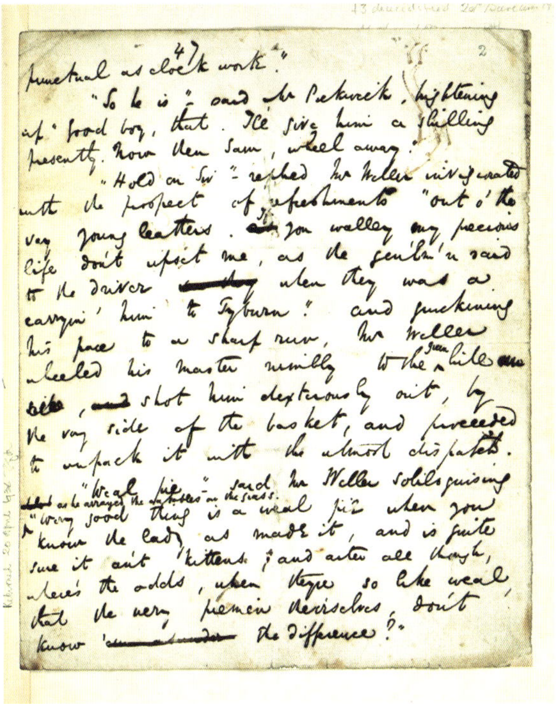

Manuscript for part of chapter 19 of *The Pickwick Papers* by Charles Dickens, 1836–37, British Library Add MS 39182, f 2r.

《匹克威克外传》第 19 章部分手稿，查尔斯·狄更斯作，1836 年至 1837 年。大英图书馆藏：Add MS 39182，f 2r.

While some writers like Charlotte Brontë produced 'fair copy' or neat manuscripts to send to the printers, Dickens sent his working drafts complete with corrections and crossings out. Once at the printers, Bradbury and Evans, compositors would work with the manuscript and select letters, called 'moveable type' and assemble blocks of text from which pages could be printed. One compositor complained of the 'thick, spluttering, blue ink, quill-penned manuscript' used by Dickens. The amount of corrections and the composition of the page suggests that Dickens worked quickly, making changes as he went along. The printed version of the story corresponds almost exactly to the text in

夏洛蒂·勃朗特等作家寄给出版社的稿子通常是誊写本或工整的手稿；而狄更斯呈交的稿件却布满了修改和圈涂的痕迹。当时负责出版狄更斯作品的布拉德伯里与伊万斯出版公司的排字工人会根据手稿内容选择相对应的字母，也就是"活字"，并将文字内容拼成版面以供印刷。一位排字工人曾抱怨狄更斯"用羽毛笔蘸着浓重的蓝墨水，写得手稿四处溅墨"。不过从该页的大量的改动和页面呈现可以看出狄更斯创作速度飞快，一边写一边改的风格。同时，作品的印刷版本与手稿的

this manuscript which shows the printers would have worked from these very sheets. This explains why so few manuscripts of *The Pickwick Papers* survive, because they were used in the printing studio and probably thrown away afterwards. Other manuscript fragments exist for *The Pickwick Papers*. Some are in the Berg Collection, New York Public Library (chapter 28), the Dickens House Museum in London, the Rosenbach Museum in Philadelphia, and the Morgan Library in New York. This manuscript is bound with a letter from an early owner, Richard Carbery. The letter is headed 13 Beaufort Buildings on the Strand, London, near where the Savoy Hotel now stands. This was the address of the solicitors firm Tyas & Tyas and it is likely that Carbery worked here. The 1851 census records a Richard Carbery who was a managing clerk to solicitors, living in Lambeth, London. He also had a brother, Henry Carbery, who was a reader at a printer's firm. Writing in 1870, Richard Carbery stated that he had owned the Pickwick manuscript for 32 years. It is not clear how Carbery obtained the manuscript in 1838 but it might have come to him from his brother's printing connections. Carbery sold the manuscript to A.J. Lewis in 1870. It was subsequently presented by Dame Alice Sedgwick Wernher, later Lady Ludlow, to be sold at the Red Cross Sale at Christie's Auctioneers in April 1915 (lot 1550) where the British Museum Library (now the British Library) purchased it for £450.

内容几乎吻合，表明很可能当时印刷作坊所用的就是这份手稿。这也解释了为什么《匹克威克外传》只有一小部分手稿得以流传——因为手稿都被寄到印刷作坊，可能用过之后就被扔掉了。作品其他的残留手稿分别藏于纽约公共图书馆中的伯格收藏（第28章）、伦敦狄更斯故居博物馆、费城罗森巴赫博物馆和纽约摩根图书馆。

与这份手稿装订在一起的还有一封信，来自于手稿曾经的所有者理查德·卡伯里。信纸上的地址是伦敦斯特兰德大街的博福特大楼，也就是现在萨沃伊酒店附近。这曾是特雅思律师事务所的所在地，卡伯里可能曾在这里工作。1851年的人口普查记录显示，有位名叫理查德·卡伯里的人是律师的管理书记员，住在伦敦的朗伯斯区。他的兄弟亨利·卡伯里是普林特斯出版公司的审稿人。理查德·卡伯里在这封写于1870年的信中称其已将《匹克威克外传》的手稿保存了32年。至于卡伯里是如何在1838年得到手稿的，我们还不清楚，有可能是通过他兄弟在出版业的关系。1870年，卡伯里将手稿卖给A.J.路易斯，之后又先后转手至爱丽丝·塞奇威克·沃纳女爵、勒德洛女士。1915年4月，在佳士得拍卖行举行的红十字会特拍中，手稿由大英博物馆图书馆，也就是如今的大英图书馆，以450英镑拍得（拍品号1550）。

狄更斯作品在中国
Charles Dickens' works in China

　　狄更斯是在中国译介最早、影响最大的英国作家之一。自 20 世纪初以来，其作品的翻译出版几乎从未间断，在一定程度上反映了 20 世纪外国文学介绍、研究的发展历程。清末民初，中国对欧美文学的译介、研究尚处于草创阶段，这一时期的狄更斯作品译本往往偏重原著大众性、娱乐性的一面，对原文多有增删以至"归化"，文字大多采用文言，尽量照顾中国读者的传统欣赏习惯，但其筚路蓝缕之功自不可磨灭。20 世纪三四十年代，随着新文学运动的兴起和外国文学研究的深入，狄更斯作品的译介空前活跃，译文也都基本改用白话，更忠实于原著，同时对狄更斯作品的研究、评论也逐渐增多，呈现出系统化、学术化的发展方向。1949 年后，狄更斯作为 19 世纪西方批判现实主义的代表作家，依然受到翻译界、研究界的重视。改革开放之后，狄更斯作品的译介更是出现了前所未有的繁荣局面，不仅已有定评的优秀译本不断再版，以往未曾翻译的作品陆续有译本问世，还出现了众多重译本，可见其受中国读者欢迎的程度。而《狄更斯文集》《狄更斯全集》等大型作品集的出版，更是堪称狄更斯作品百年译介史的辉煌总结。

作品译介

Translations

匹克威克先生在中国
Mr Pickwick in China

《旅行笑史》，常觉、小蝶译，天虚我生
润文，中华书局，1918 年。
Lü Xing Xiao Shi (*The Pickwick
Papers*), trans. by Li Changjue, Chen
Xiaodie and polished by Chen Xu,
Zhonghua Book Company, 1918.

《旅行笑史》译者照片，《新声》杂志第
三期，1921 年。
Portraits of the translators, on *Xin
Sheng Magazine* (*New Voice*), No. 3,
1921.

　　目前所知《匹克威克外传》的最早译本是"鸳鸯蝴蝶派"作家李常觉、陈小蝶与陈小蝶
之父、名作家、实业家陈栩（陈蝶仙、天虚我生）合作译述的《旅行笑史》。此译本 1918 年
由中华书局初版，仅包含原著前十九章。1921 年至 1922 年，又在《新声》杂志续刊译文九章
（内容相当于原著第二十至三十二章）。这部译本对原作颇多删节、改写，而对于滑稽逗趣的情
节、描写不仅基本完整译出，还经常"添油加醋"。类似的强调情节性、娱乐性的做法在狄更
斯作品其他早期译本中也并不鲜见，体现了典型的通俗文学趣味。

 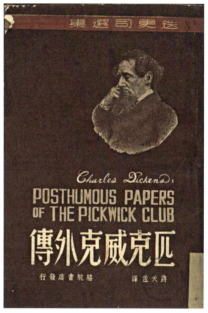

《匹克维克遗稿》，许天虹译，战地图书出
版社，1945。
The Pickwick Papers, trans. by Xu
Tianhong, War Zone Book Press, 1945.

《匹克威克外传》，蒋天佐译，骆驼书店，
1947～1948年。
The Pickwick Papers, trans. by Jiang
Tianzuo, Camel Book Company, 1947–48.

    抗战时期，许天虹在大后方翻译了《匹克维克遗稿》。1943 年，他在福建出版的《改进》
杂志发表了小说插话《古怪的当事人》的译文，并附介绍文章《关于迭更司和"匹克维克遗
稿"》。然而由于战事阻隔，译本无法按原定计划由文化生活出版社出版，只能在 1945 年 11 月
在上饶先印行了前四章译稿。抗战末期，蒋天佐在上海也开始翻译《匹克威克外传》，其间经
过被日军宪兵队逮捕、抗战胜利等事件，到 1947 年终于完成，由上海骆驼书店列为《迭更司
选集》之一出版。1949 年后经修订，又屡次重版，成为这部小说影响最大的译本。

狄更斯作品译介的先驱——林纾、魏易
The pioneers of the translation of Dickens' works: Lin Shu and Wei Yi

 早在《匹克威克先生》"远渡重洋"之前，狄更斯的其他重要作品已经被译介到了中国。1907 ～ 1909 年间，林纾与口译者魏易合作，以文言译出了《滑稽外史》(《尼古拉斯·尼克尔贝》)、《孝女耐儿传》(《老古玩店》)、《块肉余生述》(《大卫·科波菲尔》)、《贼史》(《奥立弗·退斯特》)、《冰雪因缘》(《董贝父子》) 等五部狄更斯小说，由商务印书馆列入《欧美名家小说》丛书。

林译狄更斯小说五种封面书影
The covers of Dickens' five novels, translated by Lin Shu

最近逝世之中国文学家　林纾

《最近逝世之中国文学家：林纾》,《小说月报》第十五卷第十一期，1924 年。
'The Recently Deceased Chinese Man of Letters: Lin Shu', *The Short Story Magazine*, Vol. 15, No. 11, 1924.

　　林纾（1852～1924），字琴南，号畏庐，别署冷红生、补柳翁等，福建闽县（今福州）人，是清末民初著名的古文家、翻译家。清光绪八年（1882）举人。曾先后在杭州东城讲舍、北京金台书院、京师大学堂等处任教。1897 年，林纾与留法归来的王寿昌合作，由王寿昌口译，林纾笔录润色，翻译了小仲马《巴黎茶花女遗事》，1899 年出版后大获成功。此后林纾又陆续与魏易等多位口译者合作，用文言译述了 170 余种外国文学作品，其中《黑奴吁天录》（斯陀夫人《汤姆叔叔的小屋》）、《撒克逊劫后英雄略》（司各特《艾凡赫》）、《块肉余生述》等尤负盛名，对西方文学在中国的传播做出了不可磨灭的贡献。

　　林纾虽然不懂外语，只能与口译者合作翻译，却凭借敏锐的文学眼光颇能把握原著精髓。他自述译介狄更斯小说的目的不仅在于供读者欣赏消遣，更是希望狄更斯笔下揭露的维多利亚时代英国社会的种种弊端能令国人认识到"但实力加以教育，则社会亦足改良"（《块肉余生述》序），进而"举社会中积弊，著为小说，用告当事"（《贼史》序），为维新事业添一助力。林译小说在清末至民国时期风靡一时，不断再版，甚至还出现了以林译本为蓝本的白话译本，可见其受读者欢迎的程度。林纾所确定的"迭更司"也成为 1949 年前最为通行的译名。

　　在狄更斯作品的译介史上，与林纾合作的口译者魏易也是一位不可忽略的人物。魏易（1880～1932），字春叔，浙江仁和（今杭州）人。早年在上海圣约翰大学学习。他在短短两三年间就帮助林纾译出了狄更斯五部有代表性的长篇小说，可见他同样具备相当的文学眼光。此后魏易独自以文言节译了狄更斯的另一部名著《双城记》，最初名为《二城故事》，1913年至1914年陆续刊登于《庸言》杂志；1928年自刊出版单行本《双城故事》，1933年又曾再版。1930年上海民强书店曾将原本竖排改为横排刊行。魏易去世后，上海出版商又将此译本改题"海上室主译"出版，仅在1936年至1940年间就由"锦文堂书局"（1936）、"新明书店"（1938）、"合众书店"（1940）等印行数次（实为同版重印），在当时具有一定影响。

《二城故事》，魏易译，《庸言》杂志第一卷第十三号，1913年。
A Tale of Two Cities, trans. by Wei Yi, *Yong Yan*, Vol. 1, No. 13, 1913.

狄更斯作品的其他早期译本
Other early translations of Dickens' works

　　继出版林译狄更斯小说之后，商务印书馆又在1910年出版了薛一谔、陈家麟翻译的《亚媚女士别传》，在民国初年又曾再版数次。这一译本共三十三章，相当于原著上部的内容。与林纾译著类似的是，《亚媚女士别传》同样采用文言，书名也像林译《孝女耐儿传》一样，强调主角亚媚（Amy Dorrit），采用中国旧有名称"别传"。可能是为了适应中国读者的欣赏习惯，书中对原著中长篇描写、对话常有节略，译文中多用传统辞藻，显示出强烈的"归化"倾向。

《亚媚女士别传》（《小杜丽》），薛一谔、陈家麟译，
商务印书馆，1910年。
Ya Mei Nü Shi Bie Zhuan (*Little Dorrit*), trans. by Xue
Yi'e and Chen Jialin, the Commercial Press, 1910.

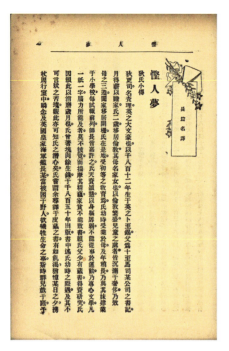

《悭人梦》，竞生译，《小说时报》第廿一号，1914 年。
Qian Ren Meng (*A Christmas Carol*), trans. by Jing Sheng, *Xiao Shuo Shi Bao*, No. 21, 1914.

1843 年发表的中篇小说《圣诞欢歌》是狄更斯影响最大的作品之一，这部批判自私冷酷、歌颂仁爱精神的作品在英语国家脍炙人口，极大地影响了近代西方的圣诞节庆传统。这篇小说目前所知的最早译本是竞生译《悭人梦》，刊登于 1914 年《小说时报》第廿一号，前附《狄氏小传》；1915 年，孙毓修摘译情节梗概，题为《耶稣诞日赋》，作为《欧美小说丛谈》中的一节发表于《小说月报》，后收入《欧美小说丛谈》单行本。1919 年，正在北京女子高等师范学校读书的女作家苏梅（苏雪林）戏仿林纾笔调节译了《圣诞欢歌》中穷雇员 Cratchit 全家圣诞晚餐一段，题为《客来及特之耶苏圣诞节》，发表于《北京女子高等师范文艺会刊》。

《鬼史》，闻宥译，上海东卓兄弟图书馆，1919 年。
Gui Shi (*A Christmas Carol*), trans. by Wen You, Shanghai Dongfu Brothers' Library, 1919.

王仲群口述、闻宥笔译的文言译本《鬼史》是目前所知《圣诞欢歌》最早的单行译本。闻宥（1901～1985），松江泗泾人，曾在申报馆、商务印书馆工作，加入南社，后来成为著名的语言学家。此译本作序者胡朴安、题签者刘三也是南社的重要成员。1924 年由上海泰西图书局再版，改题《破天荒之怪事说鬼奇闻》。

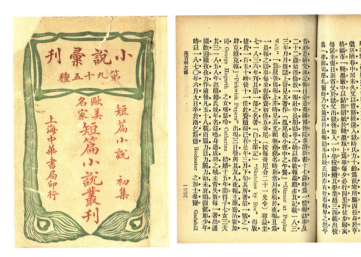

《星》，周瘦鹃译，《欧美名家短篇小说丛刊》，中华书局。
'A Child's Dream of a Star', trans. by Zhou Shoujuan, in *Short Stories by Famous European and American Writers*, Zhonghua Book Company.

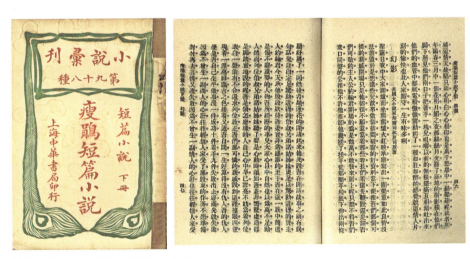

《幻影》，周瘦鹃译，《瘦鹃短篇小说》，中华书局。
'The Poor Relation's Story', trans. by Zhou Shoujuan, in *Short Stories by Shou Juan*, Zhonghua Book Company.

　　同样在民国初年，"鸳鸯蝴蝶派"名作家周瘦鹃也翻译了《至情》《星》《幻影》《前尘》等狄更斯的中短篇小说，除《幻影》采用白话之外，各篇都用文言翻译。《星》《前尘》还附有狄更斯生平、创作的简介，在狄更斯作品译介史上也占有一席之地。此外《星》在这一时期还有烟桥、佩玉译文，发表于《妇女杂志》第四卷第七号。

从文言到白话，从"译述"到直译
From classical to vernacular Chinese, from paraphrase to literary translation

《劳苦世界》(《艰难时世》)，伍光建译，商务印书馆，1926 年。
Lao Ku Shi Jie—Hard Times, trans. by Wu Guangjian, the Commercial Press, 1926.

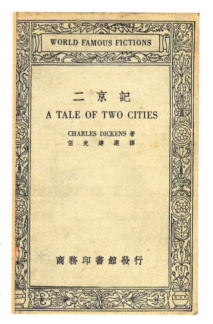

《二京记》(英汉对照)，伍光建选译，商务印书馆，1934 年。
Er Jing Ji (*A Tale of Two Cities*), a bilingual edition trans. and abridged by Wu Guangjian, the Commercial Press, 1934.

　　伍光建是近代著名的翻译家，他翻译的《劳苦世界》虽然仍多删节，但译文纯用白话，酣畅流利，颇能传神。译序虽然简短，却准确概括了这部小说的结构严谨，批判功利主义，"尊重德性"等基本特点，体现出对狄更斯及其作品的深刻理解。20 世纪 30 年代，伍光建还曾为商务印书馆编辑选译了一系列"英汉对照名家小说选"，其中的《二京记》(《双城记》)选译了原著第一部第五、六章，第三部第九、十、十二、十五章等重要章节，前附"传略"，简述狄更斯生平。

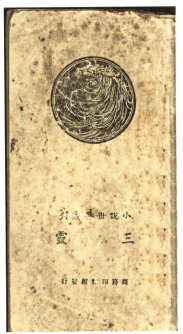
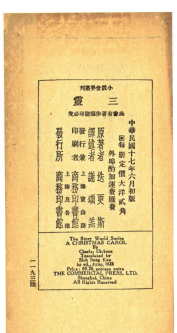

《三灵》，谢颂羔译，商务印书馆，
1928 年。
San Ling（*A Christmas Carol*），
trans. by Xie Songgao, the
Commercial Press，1928.

　　谢颂羔、米星如译《三灵》是目前所知《圣诞欢歌》最早的白话单行译本。1928 年由商
务印书馆出版。"一·二八"事变后，译者买回版权，修订译文后由基督教出版机构广学会出
版。新版译序中特别强调了原作意在劝善救世的宗教寓言性质。广学会还在 1925 年出版了李
志实根据狄更斯原著改编的剧本《圣诞之梦》。

"艰难时世"中的狄更斯作品译介

Translation of Dickens' works in 'Hard Times'

《大卫·高柏菲尔》，许天虹译，文化生活出版社，1943 年。
David Copperfield, trans. by Xu Tianhong, Cultural Life Press, 1943.

《双城记》，许天虹译，平津书店，1947 年。
A Tale of Two Cities, trans. by Xu Tianhong, Pin Jin Book Company, 1947.

　　20 世纪 40 年代，在抗战、内战接踵而至的动荡时局中，狄更斯作品的译介反而出现了前所未有的活跃局面。如许天虹在抗战期间翻译了《大卫·高柏菲尔》，其中《我的家庭生活》一章 1943 年发表于《改进》杂志，全书则在 1943 年至 1945 年间陆续由文化生活出版社作为"《迭更司选集》之一"分册出版。同期他翻译的《双城记》片断《城里的贵人》《乡间的贵人》先后刊登于《现代文艺》(1941)、《文艺丛刊》(1943) 杂志，全书于 1945 年至 1946 年同样由文化生活出版社列入《迭更司选集》出版，后来又由上海平津书店重版。

《黄昏的故事》，邹绿芷译，自强出版社，
1944 年。
A Twilight Story, trans. by Zou Lüzhi,
Ziqiang Press, 1944.

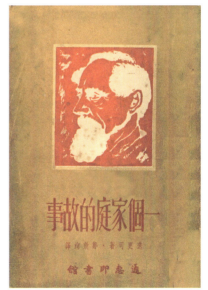

《一个家庭的故事》，邹绿芷译（误题郑效
洵译），通惠印书馆，1947 年。
The Cricket on the Hearth, trans. by Zou
Lüzhi, Tonghui Press, 1947.

　　1944 年，邹绿芷翻译的《黄昏的故事》由重庆自强出版社出版，收录了《黑面幕》《酒徒
之死》《街灯夫》《黄昏的故事》《敏斯先生及其从兄》《和雷细奥·斯帕金斯》六篇小说，1946
年又两次再版。书前附《狄更司，英国伟大的讽刺家》一文，主要概述了狄更斯作品在俄国、
苏联的传播与影响。他在抗战时期翻译的中篇小说《一个家庭的故事》(《炉边蟋蟀》) 则在
1947 年出版。

  1945 年 2 月，方敬翻译的《圣诞欢歌》由重庆文化生活出版社出版。在后记中，译者不仅肯定了狄更斯"为新的人出现而讴歌，召唤着真正人的欢乐与完美"，更希望"中国自己的'胜利欢歌'"能够"在男男女女老老少少的口里都唱起来"，展现出对于抗战胜利的热忱希望。同样在抗战胜利之际的 1945 年，陈原翻译的《人生的战斗》也由国际文化服务社在重庆出版。

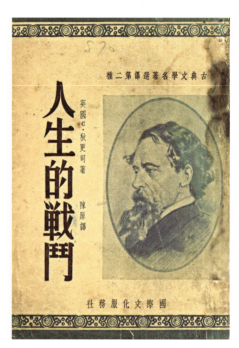

《人生的战斗》，陈原译，国际文化服务社，1947 年再版。
The Battle of Life, trans. by Chen Yuan, International Cultural Service Press，1947.

《圣诞欢歌》，方敬译，文化生活出版社，1945 年。
A Christmas Carol, trans. by Fang Jing, Cultural Life Press，1945.

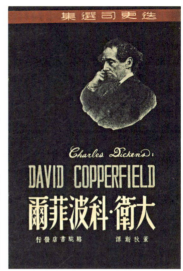

骆驼书店版《迭更司选集》。
Selected Works of Charles Dickens，
published by Camel Book Company.

　　20 世纪 40 年代，狄更斯作品的译本在数量增加、趋向忠实的同时，开始出现了较为系统的译介出版计划。早在抗战后期，仍在大后方的文化生活出版社就曾计划出版《迭更司选集》，但在出版了许天虹译《大卫·高柏菲尔自述》《双城记》以及莫洛亚《迭更司评传》之后，因种种原因未能继续。1947 年至 1948 年间，上海骆驼书店以《迭更司选集》名义先后出版了蒋天佐译《匹克威克外传》、罗稷南译《双城记》、董秋斯译《大卫·科波菲尔》、蒋天佐译《奥列佛尔》等，它们在"信达雅"等方面比起之前的各种译本都有了显著的提高，标志着狄更斯作品的译介达到了一个新的水平。1949 年后，这几种译本多次再版，继续流行，至今仍然颇有影响。

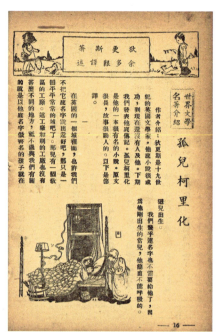

《孤儿柯里化》(节译连载)，余多艰、英冰若译，《新儿童》，1945 ～ 1947 年。
Oliver Twist, trans. and abridged by Yu Duojian and Ying Bingruo, fortnightly serial in *New Children*, 1945–47.

　　20 世纪 40 年代，狄更斯作品在中国的影响日渐深入。例如 1945 年至 1947 年的《新儿童》杂志上，就曾经连载过《孤儿柯里化》(《奥立弗·退斯特》)、《大期望》(《远大前程》) 这两部较为适合儿童阅读的狄更斯小说的部分章节，译文尽量追求浅显易懂，以适应儿童的理解能力。

1949 年后译介繁荣局面的继续
Continuation of translation after 1949

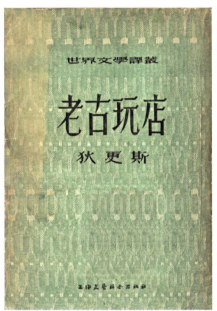

《老古玩店》，许君远译，上海文艺联合出版社，1955 年。
The Old Curiosity Shop, trans. by Xu Junyuan, Shanghai Literature and Arts United Press, 1955.

《艰难时世》，全增嘏、胡文淑译，新文艺出版社，1957 年。
Hard Times, trans. by Quan Zenggu and Hu Wenshu, New Literature and Arts Press, 1957.

《游美札记》，张谷若译，上海文艺出版社，1963 年。
American Notes, trans. by Zhang Guruo, Shanghai Literature and Arts Press, 1963.

　　1949 年后，对狄更斯作品的翻译出版在数量上进一步扩大。不仅 20 世纪 40 年代问世的一些译本得以修订再版，还出现了若干新译本。例如许君远译《老古玩店》（1955），吴钧陶、汪倜然分别翻译、同年（1955）出版的两种《圣诞欢歌》译本，高殿森译《着魔的人》（1955），金福译《钟乐》（1956），全增嘏、胡文淑译《艰难时世》（1957），张谷若译《游美札记》（1963），等等。同时问世的还有几种节译本，如林汉达译《大卫·考柏飞》（1951）、熊友榛译《雾都孤儿》等。在这一时期，"Dickens"的译法逐渐由"迭更司""狄根斯"等统一为"狄更斯"。

狄更斯作品译介的全盛时期
The boom period of the translation of Dickens' works

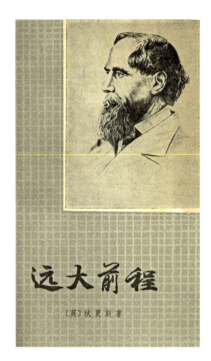

《远大前程》，王科一译，上海译文出版社，
1979 年。
Great Expectations, trans. by Wang Keyi,
Shanghai Translation Publishing House,
1979.

《荒凉山庄》，黄邦杰、陈少衡、张自谋译，上
海译文出版社，1979 年。
Bleak House, trans. by Huang Bangjie, Chen
Shaoheng and Zhang Zimou, Shanghai
Translation Publishing House, 1979.

《狄更斯文集》（19 卷），上海译文出版社，1998 年。
Collected Works of Charles Dickens，19 vols.
Shanghai Translation Publishing House, 1998.

　　"文革"之后，20 世纪 70 年代末重新公开出版的第一批外国文学名著中就包括了董秋斯译《大卫·科波菲尔》，全增嘏、胡文淑译《艰难时世》，蒋天佐译《匹克威克外传》等。从此开始，随着文化事业的复苏和出版事业的繁荣，此前已有定评的各种狄更斯作品译本不断重印，此前未曾完整译介的作品译本、各种重译本也陆续出版，几乎难以计数。仅上海译文出版社就陆续推出了王科一译《远大前程》（1979），黄邦杰、陈少衡、张自谋译《荒凉山庄》（1979），张谷若译《大卫·考坡菲》（1980），叶维之译《马丁·瞿述伟》（1983），荣如德译《奥立弗·退斯特》（1984），金绍禹译《意大利风光》（1985），智量译《我们共同的朋友》（1986），项星耀译《德鲁德疑案》（1986），张玲、张扬译《双城记》（1989），高殿森、程海波、高清正译《巴纳比·鲁吉》（1990），项星耀译《中短篇小说选》（1991），陈漪、西海译《博兹特写集》（1992），金绍禹译《小杜丽》（1993），祝庆英译《董贝父子》（1994），杜南星、徐文绮译《尼古拉斯·尼克尔贝》（1998），等等。1998 年汇编为《狄更斯文集》19 卷出版，这是当时最为权威完备的狄更斯作品中译版本。2012 年狄更斯诞辰 200 周年之际，浙江工商大学出版社又推出了《狄更斯全集》24 卷，收录了狄更斯的全部作品，其中《演讲集》《戏剧、诗歌、短篇小说集》《非旅行推销商札记》《重印集》《儿童英国史》等五部作品是第一次被介绍到中国。这两部大型作品集的翻译出版，可谓狄更斯作品在中文世界百余年译介历程的辉煌总结。

评论研究
Reviews

《史传：英国二大小说家迭根斯及萨克礼略传》，《大陆报》第二卷第十二期，1904 年。
'A Biographical Sketch of Two Great British Novelists: Dickens and Thackeray', *Da Lu Magazine*, Vol. 2, No. 12, 1904.

目前所知中文世界最早出现的狄更斯评介文章是 1904 年《大陆报》刊载的《史传：英国二大小说家迭根斯及萨克礼略传》，此文称狄更斯、萨克雷为"輓近英国有二大小说家，远超乎流辈之上"，概略介绍了狄更斯的生平与创作成就。虽然内容较为简短，却标志着狄更斯评介研究在中国的发端。

林纾《块肉余生述》译序
Preface to *Kuai Rou Yu Sheng Shu* (*David Copperfield*) by Lin Shu

　　林纾不仅是系统译介狄更斯作品的第一人，他在译序、评语中还对狄更斯的创作成就给予了高度评价。他尤其推崇狄更斯"极力抉摘下等社会之积弊"（《贼史》序）的批判精神，"奸侩驵酷，至于人意未所尝置想之局，幻为空中楼阁，使观者或笑或怒，一时颠倒，至于不能自已"（《孝女耐儿传》序）的生动笔力，以及"如善奕之著子，偶然一下，不知后来咸得其用"（《块肉余生述》序）的精妙布局，认为其文学成就远在自己译介的另两位名作家司各得、小仲马之上（《冰雪因缘》序），甚至不亚于"左（丘明）、（司）马（迁）、班（固）、韩（愈）"等古文大家和《石头记》这样最杰出的中国小说。

孙毓修《欧美小说丛谈：司各德、迭更斯二家之批评》,《小说月报》第四卷第三期, 1913 年。

'Remarks on European and American Fictions: A Review on Walter Scott and Charles Dickens' by Sun Yuxiu, *The Short Story Magazine*, Vol. 4, No. 3, 1913.

民国初年，孙毓修编写的《欧美小说丛谈》在《小说月报》连载发表，1916 年 12 月由商务印书馆出版单行本。书中《司各德、迭更斯二家之批评》一章简要介绍了狄更斯的生平、创作，认为"世界众生之行乐图，无古无今，悉为此老写尽矣"。文末引述"英人"之说，将狄更斯与莎士比亚、司各特并称为英国三大文豪，"别国文学史，无能与此三人并对之人物"，肯定了狄更斯在英国文学史上的崇高地位。

谢六逸《西洋小说发达史》五《自然主义时代》（中），《小说月报》第十三卷第六期，1922 年。
A History of the Development of Western Fiction by Xie Liuyi, Chapter 5 'Age of Naturalism' Section 2, *The Short Story Magazine*, Vol. 13, No. 6, 1922.

郑振铎《文学大纲》第二十八章《十九世纪的英国小说》，《小说月报》第十七卷第六期，1926 年。
The Outline of Literature by Zheng Zhenduo, Chapter 28 'British Fictions in the 19th Century', *The Short Story Magazine*, Vol. 17, No. 6, 1926.

20 世纪二三十年代出版的几种世界文学史著作对于狄更斯的生平、创作也都有所论述，如谢六逸《西洋小说发达史》述及狄更斯生前已经"称为英伦第一小说家"，认为他"是一个理想家，是一个社会改良家"，可以和巴尔扎克相比；郑振铎《文学大纲》则较为全面地介绍了狄更斯的生平和主要作品，概括了狄更斯擅长塑造社会中下层人物、批判"社会的制度与组织"、风格"真切而朴素"、善于吸引读者同感等创作特点。又如曾虚白《英国文学 ABC》、金东雷《英国文学史纲》等文学史著都为狄更斯专辟章节，详细论述。

《译文》新三卷第一期《迭更司特辑》，1937 年。
Special Issue on Charles Dickens, *Yi Wen* (*Translations*), Vol. 3, No. 1, 1937.

[法] 莫洛亚《迭更司评传》，许天虹译，文化生活出版社，1943 年。
Dickens by André Maurois, trans. by Xu Tianhong, Cultural Life Press, 1943.

　　20 世纪三四十年代，左翼文学阵营同样十分重视对狄更斯作品的评介。例如鲁迅、茅盾创办的《译文》杂志就在 1935 年刊登了梅格凌（弗朗茨·梅林）的《狄更斯论》；1937 年又推出"迭更司特辑"，刊登了许天虹翻译的苏联学者亚尼克尼斯德的《迭更司论——为人道而战的现实主义大师》及法国评论家莫洛亚《迭更司评传》中的篇章。许天虹此后又翻译了《迭更司评传》中的《迭更司的哲学》，刊登于《现代文艺》1941 年第二卷第六期。1943 年，《迭更司评传》单行本由桂林文化生活出版社出版。这是 1949 年之前翻译出版的唯一一部狄更斯研究专著。

高倚筠《狄更斯的"耶稣传"》,《新垒》第四卷第五期,
1934 年。
'*The Life of Our Lord* by Charles Dickens', by Gao Yiyun,
New Fort，Vol. 4，No. 5，1934.

　　值得一提的是，狄更斯去世 64 年后才首次出版的遗著《耶稣传》在 20 世纪三四十年代
也引起了中国文学界、宗教界的注意。早在 1934 年此书出版后不久,《新垒》杂志第四卷第五
期就发表了高倚筠的评介文章《狄更斯的"耶稣传"》，不仅叙述了这部作品写作、流传、出
版的经过，更借此探讨了狄更斯、安诺德等英国维多利亚时代文学家的宗教观。1947 年，基
督教刊物《天风》第七十五期也刊登了林永俣《狄更斯写给他自己孩子们读的耶稣传》一文。
在此前后，此书有不止一种译本面世 [1]。

1　《耶稣传》，薛诚之译，东方书社，1946 年；《耶稣传》，方木译，天主教教务协进委员会，1950 年。

《狄更斯评论集》，罗经国编，上海译文出版社，1981年。
Charles Dickens: A Collection of Critical Sources, ed. by Luo Jingguo, Shanghai Translation Publishing House, 1981.

薛鸿时《浪漫的现实主义：狄更斯评传》，社会科学文献出版社，1996年。
The Romantic Realism: A Critical Biography of Charles Dickens by Xue Hongshi, Social Sciences Academic Press（China），1996.

[英]阿克罗伊德《狄更斯传》，包雨苗译，北京师范大学出版社，2007年。
Dickens by Peter Ackroyd, trans. by Bao Yumiao, Beijing Normal University Press, 2007.

　　20世纪后半期，中国的狄更斯研究起先在五六十年代受苏联影响，主要重视狄更斯作品中对社会黑暗的揭露批判，同时指出其"阶级局限性"。改革开放之后，对狄更斯作品的评论、研究进入前所未有的高潮，出现了众多专著；与此同时，对国外狄更斯传记、研究著作的引进、译介也十分发达，呈现出"百花齐放"的繁荣局面。

一本狄更斯藏书的奇妙旅行
Adventures of a book from Gads Hill Place

狄更斯的私人藏书《中国第二次战役纪行》书名页与藏书票。
The Exlibris of Charles Dickens from one of his book collection, *Narrative of the Second Compaign in Chin*a, now in Shanghai Library.

　　从小喜爱翻阅父亲藏书的查尔斯·狄更斯，对书籍也有着深刻的热爱。在盖兹山庄的图书室内，狄更斯收藏了大量各类主题的图书。内有狄更斯的私人藏书票：手握马耳他十字的雄狮。这一形象可以追溯到狄更斯家族 17 世纪的某位先祖使用的纹章。

　　在上海图书馆收藏的外文藏书中，有一册《中国第二次战役纪行》(*Narrative of the Second Compaign in China*)，其封二就贴有这张藏书票。此书出版于 1842 年，记录了第一次鸦片战争中英国军队在中国的军事行动与政治动态。封二还有一张标签，记录此书入藏盖兹山庄的时间为 1870 年。

　　此书之后不知经过了如何奇妙的旅行，流入了中国，被原耶稣会徐家汇藏书楼收藏，现为上海图书馆馆藏，成为中西交流的见证。

阅读狄更斯简史

肖一之

　　查尔斯·约翰·赫法姆·狄更斯（1812～1870）应该是19世纪最著名的英国小说家了。在狄更斯活着的时候，他的作品就广受读者的欢迎和评论界的好评。在去世后狄更斯更是获得了安葬西敏寺"诗人角"的荣耀，这更进一步奠定了他身后的声誉。狄更斯被英国著名的评论家F.R.里维斯和Q.D.里维斯夫妇赞颂为"最伟大的创意作家之一"，而且他到今天都还在吸引着世界各地的读者，他的作品也为无数的戏剧、电视剧和电影提供了灵感，可以说围绕着狄更斯诞生了一个完整的文化产业。狄更斯也和莎士比亚以及简·奥斯丁一起成为了英国文学最为人熟知的代表。

　　然而当狄更斯1812年出生在一个海军小职员家庭的时候，没有任何迹象显示他将来会如此知名。狄更斯的父亲不善理财——评论家们认为《大卫·科波菲尔》里友善但是糊涂的米考伯先生的原型就是他的父亲——以至于狄更斯家一度堕入贫困，狄更斯幼年甚至不得不在工厂工作过一段时间。15岁的时候狄更斯就离开了学校，在短暂地当了一段时间法律事务所的文员之后成为了一名记者。1836年，《博兹札记》的出版让他尝到了文学事业上的首次成功。1837年出版的《匹克威客外传》更是让他一夜成名。他辞去了记者的工作，从此开始全身心投入到写作事业中。狄更斯一生非常多产，在他去世的时候，他留下了十好几部小说，篇目繁多的短篇故事，几部戏剧和包括西德尼·卡尔顿、小杜丽、郝薇香小姐和奥利弗·特威斯特在内众多脍炙人口的文学形象。

　　在狄更斯去世的时候，人们记得的不光是这些栩栩如生的人物形象的创造者；对当时的公众来说，狄更斯的离世更像是一位不仅为他们仗义执言也为他们提供慰藉的老朋友猝然早逝了。

　　在他的文学生涯中，狄更斯从来没有回避过自己写作的社会责任。在他的小说里，他谴责了《济贫法》的残酷，讽刺了英国官僚的腐化，为公共卫生改革呐喊，也在一个越来越感受到工业化生产和消费重压的时代里歌颂了人类情谊的宝贵。再没有比饥饿的奥利弗·特威斯特举起碗想再吃一碗燕麦粥的场景更能揭露《济贫法》所带来的苦难，也再没有比《荒凉山庄》里那场不分贵贱一律抹杀的传染病更能说明卫生改革的急迫了。狄更斯的社会影响是如此之大以至于他的儿子亨利·菲尔丁·狄更斯回忆说在他父亲死后不久，一个出租马车夫认出了他，对他说："啊，狄更斯先生，你父亲去世是我们所有人的大损失——我们这些出租马车夫还希望他很快会做点什么来帮助我们呢。"对维多利时代的劳工阶层来说，狄更斯先生绝不仅仅是位小说家，而是几乎已经成了一种公共机构。

19世纪读者和狄更斯的紧密联系也通过狄更斯去世之后公众缅怀他的方式表现了出来。狄更斯去世之后登载的大量讣告有一个重要的特色，那就是狄更斯被描述成他所有读者的朋友。事实上，狄更斯是把握英国人感情脉动的天才，而他也把牵着英国读者追寻故事的起伏，分享故事中人物苦乐的技艺发展到了化境。因此阅读狄更斯的作品很像来到一个社交场合：作者在那里为自己的读者介绍了一个又一个的新朋友。后来成为了《泰晤士报》主编的托马斯·切纳里在《泰晤士报》上的狄更斯讣告里写道，狄更斯的去世"对成百万的人来说俨然便是丧亲之痛"。而在西敏寺举行的纪念布道里，本杰明·乔伊特则似乎替这成百万人说出了心声，他说道："人类失去的不仅仅是一位伟大的作家，而是一位他们熟识的人，一位他们和他们家人的朋友。"无论是在狄更斯之前或者之后，少有作家能够和自己的读者保持如此亲密的关系。

数码时代的我们要想象狄更斯在19世纪受欢迎的程度多少有点困难。面对其他各种娱乐方式的挑战，没有哪位当代作家可以像当年的狄更斯一样流行。在狄更斯事业的顶峰，他是维多利亚时代出版市场的霸主。当时一本小说卖到几千本就已经算是畅销了，而狄更斯小说连载的时候，每周出版的连载章节销售量动辄十几万份。当然，读者们也不是对狄更斯所有的小说都怀有如此的热情，但是对他们最爱的小说，当时读者的激情可以让所有现代的文学粉丝相形见绌。1841年的一天，载有狄更斯的《老古玩店》连载终章的轮船还没有驶入纽约港，一大群人就已经焦急地等在码头上，他们想要知道小说的女主人公小内尔在故事的结尾是否活了下来。人群根本就没有耐心等船靠岸，他们冲到码头上激动地询问内尔的最终命运。不过，狄更斯的高涨的人气却成了他在20世纪早期评论家眼里不受欢迎的原因。

"如果在半文盲里受欢迎的程度是文学声誉最稳妥的测量方式的话，那么狄更斯就肯定是英国最出类拔萃的小说家。"1888 年，弗吉尼亚·伍尔夫的父亲，英国作家莱斯利·史蒂文在他主编的《国家人物传记词典》里如此写道。仅仅在他去世之后不到 20 年，狄更斯的作品一直受到劳工阶层青睐的事实却成为了质疑他的文学价值的原因。维多利亚时代的读者热爱狄更斯的早期作品。诸如《匹克威客外传》《尼古拉斯·尼克贝》《马丁·瞿述韦》《奥利弗·特威斯特》《老古玩店》等小说吸引读者的主要原因就是它们要不是写得幽默风趣，要不就是能够让读者体会到情感上的跌宕起伏。然而，当小说逐渐在 20 世纪成为一种艺术形式的时候，评论家们对狄更斯失去了耐心。狄更斯的幽默和丰沛的情感在 20 世纪的评论家和小说家眼里就成了粗俗的笑话和扭捏作态，而他奔流张扬的写作则成了他对优秀小说的形式要求一无所知的证据。因此，在 20 世纪的前半期，狄更斯一直是普通读者热爱的作家，而被批评家们所忽略。

在 20 世纪早期，评论家们对狄更斯的兴趣降到最低点，任何胆敢研究狄更斯的学者甚至都没法在牛津或者剑桥大学找到工作。不过到了 20 世纪中叶，狄更斯终于开始时来运转了。现代作家对小说形式孜孜不倦的试验终于让评论家们认识到，狄更斯小说看似杂乱的勃勃生气并非是小说技艺的失败，而是一种独特的文学天才的表现。狄更斯的确像他自称的那样，是一位"不可模仿的伟大作家"。说明评论家们对狄更斯的态度变化最好的例子就是 F.R. 里维斯自我否定的故事。在里维斯 1948 年出版的经典英国小说史著作《伟大的传统》中，他认为作为一位"创意艺术家"，狄更斯的伟大是不容怀疑的，但是他的天才仅仅是一位"伟大的说笑话的人"。20 多年之后，在狄更斯去世 100 周年的 1970 年，里维斯在他和妻子合著的《小说家狄更斯》里全盘推翻了自己早前的断言。现在，狄更斯成了一位"深刻的、严肃的而且机智得令人惊叹的小说作者，一位大师"。自此之后，狄更斯作为一位伟大小说家的地位再也没有被质疑过。不过现代评论家们并不赞同维多利亚时代的读者选出来的狄更斯的最佳作品，而是重新开列了他们心中的狄更斯的代表作。现代评论家认为狄更斯晚期的作品才是真正重要的。《艰难时世》《荒凉山庄》《远大前程》《我们共同的朋友》这些小说才能真正展示出小说大师狄更斯的高超艺术水平。

对普通读者来说，狄更斯在文学史上的起起落落不过是背景里的争吵罢了，因为他从来没有淡出过他们的视野。在他去世将近一个半世纪之后，狄更斯依旧凭借着他的幽默、他的社会批判和他的小说艺术手法吸引了新一代的读者。在我们这个时代，纪念狄更斯的方法也不止阅读这一种。就像英国广播公司 2015 年大受欢迎的电视剧《狄更斯世界》

证明的那样，即使在我们这个读图时代，观众们也不能抗拒真正的狄更斯式故事的诱惑。而一辈子都是戏剧爱好者也是高超的表演者的狄更斯肯定会乐于看到自己的作品被改编成了各种形式。毕竟，晚年狄更斯也曾经自己动手把自己的小说改编成了大受欢迎的朗诵表演。在他的告别朗诵会的结尾，狄更斯说："现在我将永远从这刺眼的灯光下消失了。"而现在我们知道，只要还有人读书或者还有人观看表演，狄更斯就永远不会消失。

肖一之

美国布朗大学比较文学博士，主要研究19世纪英国文学、文学与科学以及英国文学在中国。现为上海外国语大学英语学院讲师。

Reading Dickens: A Short History

Xiao Yizhi

Charles John Huffam Dickens (1812–70) was probably the most famous British novelist of the 19th century. During his lifetime, Dickens' works were acknowledged by readers and critics alike. His claim to everlasting fame was further cemented by his interment in Poets' Corner in Westminster Abbey after his death. Hailed by the renowned English critics F.R. and Q.D. Leavis as 'one of the greatest of creative writers ', Dickens continues to attract readers all over the world today, with his works inspiring countless plays, TV series and films that have made him the epicenter of a veritable cultural industry. Together with Shakespeare and Jane Austen, Dickens has become one the most recognizable faces in English literature.

Few could have predicted Dickens' later fame when he was born into the family of a navy clerk in 1812. His father's financial ineptitude, which is believed to have inspired the character of the amicable yet confused Mr Micawber in *David Copperfield*, led the family to poverty, and for a short time, Dickens was forced to work in a factory. Dickens left school at 15, and after a stint as a law clerk, became a journalist. In 1836, Dickens had the first taste of literary success when his *Sketches by Boz* were published. In 1837, the publication of *The Pickwick Papers* turned Dickens into a literary sensation. He resigned from his role as a journalist and devoted himself fully to a long and productive career as a writer. At the end of his life, he would leave the world with more than a dozen novels, a large collection of short stories, several plays and a host of memorable characters including Sydney Carton, Little Dorrit, Miss Havisham, and Oliver Twist.

At the time of his death, Dickens was not just seen as the creator of life-like and popular characters; the public also saw the passing of Dickens as the untimely death of a dear old friend who spoke for them as well as consoled them.

Throughout his career, Dickens did not turn away from the social impact of his writing. In his novels, he denounced the cruelty of the Poor Law, satirized the corruption of British bureaucracy, advocated public health reform, and championed the value of human companionship in an age that was becoming increasingly aware of the harshness of mass industrial production and consumption. Nothing highlights the suffering under the Poor Law like the image of hungry Oliver Twist holding out his bowl for more porridge and nothing brings home the urgency of sanitary reform like the deadly contagious disease that killed both the rich and the poor in *Bleak House*. Dickens' social impact was such that his son, Henry Fielding Dickens, recalled that shortly after his father's death, a cabbie recognized him and said: 'Ah, Mr Dickens, your father's death was a great loss to all of us—and we cabbies were in hopes that he would soon be doing something to help us'. To the Victorian working class, Mr Dickens was so much more than a mere novelist; he was almost a public institution.

Dickens' close connection to his reading public in the 19th century also is highlighted by way they chose to remember him. Among the obituaries that poured forth after the death of the novelist, one thing was most significant: Dickens was described as a friend to all his readers. In fact, Dickens was a genius when it came to taking the pulse of the English and he perfected the skill of leading his readers through the twists and turns of his stories, making them share in the laughter and tears of the characters. Reading Dickens is not unlike a social occasion where he introduces his readers to one new friend after another. Thomas Chenery, the future editor of *The Times*, wrote in *The Times*' obituary for Dickens that his death would be felt 'by millions as nothing less than a personal bereavement'. In the memorial sermon delivered in Westminster Abbey, Benjamin Jowett seemed to speak for those millions when he said that 'Men seemed to have lost, not a great writer only, but one whom they had personally known; who was the friend of them and of their families'. Few writers, before or after Dickens, have enjoyed such an intimate relationship with his or her public.

For those of us in the digital age, it may be somewhat challenging to imagine the tremendous popularity Dickens enjoyed back in the 19th century. No contemporary author can ever hope to achieve comparable popularity against so many other forms of entertainment. However, at the peak of his career, Dickens dominated the Victorian publishing market. At a time when a novel selling a few thousand copies was considered popular, the sales of Dickens' weekly installments ranged in the 100,000s. The reading public certainly did not follow all his novels with the same enthusiasm, but when they did, they did so with a passion that would put any modern literary groupie to shame. In 1841, when the ship that carried the final installment of *The Old Curiosity Shop* reached New York, an anxious crowd was waiting there to find out whether the heroine of the story, Little Nell, survived or not in the end. They did not wait for the ship to dock, but stormed the wharf, fervently demanding to know her fate. Yet Dickens's tremendous popularity also sowed the seeds of his troubled critical reception at the turn of the 20th century.

'If literary fame could be safely measured by popularity with the half-educated, Dickens must claim the highest position among English novelists' wrote Leslie Stephen, father of Virginia Woolf, in *The Dictionary of National Biography* in 1888. Less than twenty years after his death, Dickens' unrelenting popularity with the working class became exactly the reason to question his literary value. The Victorians adored the early works of Dickens. Novels such as *The Pickwick Papers*, *Nicholas Nickleby*, *Martin Chuzzlewit*, *Oliver Twist*, and *The Old Curiosity Shop* attracted the Victorian readers because they offered either comical entertainments or an emotional roller-coaster ride. However, when novels began to claim the status of an art form in the 20th century, critics lost their patience with Dickens. His humour and pathos became, in the eyes of 20th-century critics and novelists, low comedy and mere sentimentality and his exuberant way of writing became evidence that he knew nothing about the construction of a good novel. As a result, in the first half of 20th century, Dickens remained a popular author for the general reading public yet neglected by the critical establishment.

The critical disdain for Dickens in the early part of the 20th century was such that scholars who dared to study Dickens and his works were barred from positions at Oxbridge. By the middle of the century, however, things began to come around again: the modernists' persevering investigation into form finally led critics to recognize the unruly vitality of Dickensian writing not as a failure of the craft of fiction but as the manifestations of a unique literary genius. Dickens truly was 'the Great Inimitable', as he liked to call himself. Nothing better demonstrates the shift of the critical attitude on Dickens than the changing positions of F.R. Leavis. In his 1948 classic on the history of English novels, *The Great Tradition*, Leavis wrote that as a 'creative artist ', the greatness of Dickens is certain, but his genius is nothing more than that of a 'great entertainer'. More than two decades later, on the centenary of Dickens' death in 1970, Leavis did a complete about-turn in *Dickens the Novelist*, which he co-authored with his wife, and dismissed his own earlier assessment. Dickens now was a 'profound, serious and wonderfully resourceful practicing novelist, a master of it'. After that, Dickens' position as a master of the art of the novel was never questioned again. Yet modern critics did not agree with the Victorians on which were the best novels by Dickens, and came up with their own list of works they deemed worthy of critical acclaim. To them, it was Dickens' later works that truly mattered — *Hard Times*, *Bleak House*, *Great Expectations* and *Our Mutual Friend* were works that illustrated the mastery of Dickens as a novelist.

For the common reader, the ups and downs of Dickens' literary status is a minor consideration, for he has never faded from view. Almost a century and a half after his death, Dickens still fascinates a new generation of readers with his humor, social messages, and his artistry as a novelist. In our own age, we also pay tribute to Dickens in ways other than just reading. As the popular BBC TV series *Dickensian* (2015) demonstrated, even audiences in our image-addicted age cannot resist the allure of Dickensian stories. Dickens himself, a life-long lover of the theatre and a master performer himself, would have loved the various adaptations of his works in different forms of media. After all, he adapted his novels into wildly popular recitals in his later life. At the end of his farewell recital, he said that 'from this garish light I now vanish for ever more'. Yet we know that as long as people can read books or watch performances, Dickens will never vanish.

Xiao Yizhi

Lecturer of English at Shanghai International Studies University. He received his PhD in comparative literature from Brown University in 2017. His research interests include nineteenth-century English literature, literature and science, and the dissemination and acceptance of English literature in China.

29 Nov 1915

Dear Pinker,

I am here with
Phillip Morrell & Lady Ottoline
until Friday. We are talking
about printing The Rainbow
privately, by subscription.
I really think it ought
to be done.

I wish you could appro...
Methuen — in some way

IV

大卫·赫伯特·劳伦斯

DAVID
HERBERT
LAWRENCE

Portrait of D.H. Lawrence by Elliot & Fry, bromide press print, circa 1915.

D.H. 劳伦斯肖像，埃利奥特与弗里摄影工作室摄于约 1915 年，1971 年由《每日先驱报》购得。

大卫·赫伯特·劳伦斯 是 20 世纪前期英国最杰出的小说家之一，在诗歌、散文、戏剧、文学批评以至绘画等方面也都卓有成就。1885年 9 月 11 日，他生于英国诺丁汉郡。父亲是煤矿工人，文化程度不高；母亲当过小学教师，较有文化修养。劳伦斯自幼深受母亲影响，爱好读书，1906 年至 1908 年在诺丁汉大学学习，毕业后到伦敦附近的克罗伊登教书，开始创作诗歌、小说。1911 年发表第一部长篇小说《白孔雀》，同年因患肺病辞去教职。1912 年，劳伦斯与诺丁汉大学教授威克利的德国妻子弗丽达（1879 ～ 1956）私奔，两人于 1914 年正式结婚。1913 年，劳伦斯的首部重要小说《儿子与情人》出版，奠定了他的文坛声誉。第一次世界大战期间，由于反战立场和妻子的德裔身份，劳伦斯遭到英国当局怀疑、骚扰。1915 年，长篇小说《虹》出版不久就因"诲淫"罪名被禁，续篇《恋爱中的女人》1920 年在美国出版。1919 年，劳伦斯夫妇离开英国，先后旅居意大利、澳大利亚、美国、墨西哥等国，其间劳伦斯完成了长篇小说《袋鼠》（1923）、《羽蛇》（1926）、短篇小说《骑马出走的女人》（1925）等大量作品。1925 年，劳伦斯的肺结核病情日益严重，不得不与弗丽达回到欧洲，定居意大利。1928 年，长篇小说《查泰莱夫人的情人》在意大利出版，随即在英、美等国被查禁。1929 年夏，在伦敦举办的劳伦斯个人画展也遭到警方搜查。1930年 3 月 2 日，劳伦斯在法国南部小镇旺斯的疗养院中病逝。

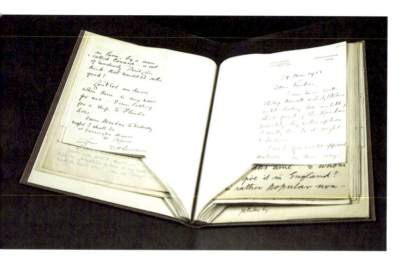

Manuscript letter from D.H. Lawrence to his agent in London, James Brand Pinker, dated 29 November 1915, from a volume of letters from Lawrence to Pinker, British Library Add MS 74258, f 27r.

D.H. 劳伦斯写给其伦敦代理人詹姆斯·布兰德·平克的亲笔信,信的日期为 1915 年 11 月 29 日,收录在一宗劳伦斯致平克的信函中。大英图书馆藏:Add MS 74258,f 27r。

This is one of 57 letters in a volume of correspondence from the writer David Herbert Lawrence (1885–1930) to his London agent, James Brand Pinker (1863–1922) which is held in the British Library. The letter of 29 November 1915 was written from the home of the patron and society hostess Lady Ottoline Morrell, Garsington Manor near Oxford. [Fig. 1] Morell was an influential friend to many writers including T.S. Eliot, whose manuscripts also feature in this publication, Aldous Huxley, Lawrence and Siegfried Sassoon. She married the Member of Parliament Philip Morrell in 1902 with whom she shared a love for the arts.

藏于大英图书馆的这封信是作家大卫·赫伯特·劳伦斯写给其伦敦代理人詹姆斯·布兰德·平克的 57 封信中的一封。写信日期为 1915 年 11 月 29 日,写于牛津附近的嘉辛顿庄园,庄园主人是奥托琳·莫瑞尔夫人(图 1)。奥托琳·莫瑞尔夫人与许多作家都是至交好友,譬如托马斯·斯特恩斯·艾略特(他的手稿也收录在本书之中)、阿道司·赫胥黎、劳伦斯以及西格夫里·萨松。她于 1902 年嫁给同样热爱艺术的议会议员菲利普·莫瑞尔。

The letter refers to Lawrence's 1915 novel, *The Rainbow*, which tells the story of three generations of a Nottinghamshire family from 1840 to 1905. The central character in the novel is the unconventional Ursula Brangwen who challenges her role as a woman in the home. Because of its sexual content and same-sex affairs, the book was seized under the 1857 Obscene Publications Act and prosecuted in an obscenity trial on 13 November 1915. Over 1000 copies were burned outside the Royal Exchange in London and it was banned and unavailable in Britain until 1926. Lawrence's letter to Pinker was written just after the trial. In it, he says 'I am here with Phillip Morrell and Lady Ottoline until Friday. We are talking about printing *The Rainbow* privately, by subscription'. [1] He continues 'I really think it ought to be done. I wish you could approach Methuen—in this way—whether ourselves, to do it'. Here, he is referring to his publisher, Methuen, whom he hopes will agree to him publishing the novel privately in Italy. Metheun had asked that *The Rainbow* undergo a serious edit before publication yet when the book was on trial, Methuen feigned innocence at knowledge of its contents.

这封信提到了劳伦斯 1915 年的小说《虹》，小说讲述了住在诺丁汉郡的一家三代 1840 年到 1905 年的遭遇。主角之一厄休拉·布兰文是一位非传统的女性，她不断反抗家庭给自己设定的女性角色。由于涉及性爱描写以及同性恋的内容，此书在 1857 年《淫秽出版物法》的规定下被禁止发行，并因淫秽内容受到起诉，于 1915 年 11 月 13 日遭审判。1000 多本《虹》在伦敦英国皇家交易所门外被烧毁。一直到 1926 年，这本书在英国都被禁止发行。劳伦斯寄给平克的信正是在这场审判之后写的。他在信中写道："我会在菲利普·莫瑞尔和奥托琳夫人的庄园待到周五。我们在商量以订购的方式私下印刷出版《虹》。"他又继续写道："我真的觉得必须得这么做。我希望您能找一下梅休因——这样试试——不管是不是我们自己来做，都要做成。"在这里提到的梅休因是劳伦斯的出版人，劳伦斯希望梅休因同意他在意大利私下发行小说的想法。在《虹》出版之前，梅休因曾要求对这本书进行认真编辑，但当法庭审判此书时，梅休因却装作对书的内容一无所知。

Fig.1

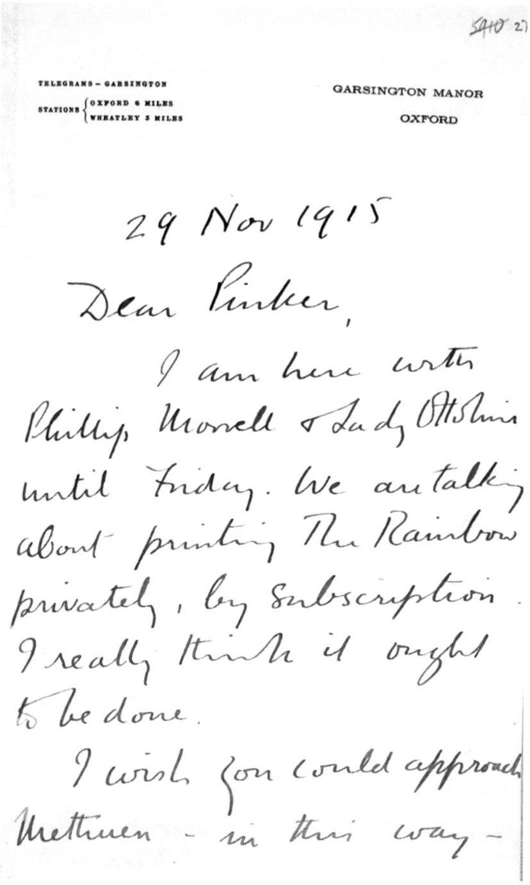

TELEGRAMS – GARSINGTON

STATIONS { OXFORD 6 MILES
           WHEATLEY 3 MILES

GARSINGTON MANOR
OXFORD

SATO 27

29 Nov 1915

Dear Pinker,

I am here with Phillip Morrell & Lady Ottoline until Friday. We are talking about printing The Rainbow privately, by subscription. I really think it ought to be done.

I wish you could approach Methuen — in this way —

Manuscript letter from D.H. Lawrence to his agent in London, James Brand Pinker, dated 29 November 1915, British Library Add MS 74258, f 27r.

D.H. 劳伦斯写给其伦敦代理人詹姆斯·布兰德·平克的亲笔信，信的日期为 1915 年 11 月 29 日，收录在一宗劳伦斯致平克的信函中。大英图书馆藏：Add MS 74258，f 27r.

Lawrence was evidently affected by the trial and in another letter to Pinker dated 6 November 1915 he wrote 'I heard yesterday about the magistrates and *The Rainbow*. I am not very much moved: am beyond that by now. I only curse them all, body and soul, root, branch and leaf, to eternal damnation'.[2] Lawrence had hoped that other authors would stage a public protest against the suppression of *The Rainbow*: 'I think it would be a really good thing to get the public protest from the authors — Bennett, etc. John Drinkwater came in just now — he is anxious to do something. Very many people are in a rage over the occurrence. Will you organize a public protest, do you think? — it would be best'.[3]

审判一事显然对劳伦斯触动很大。他在 1915 年 11 月 6 日给平克的另一封信中写道："我昨天听说了地方法院对《虹》的态度，我的情绪没怎么受影响——我现在已经超脱那些了。我只是诅咒所有这些人，从肉体到灵魂，从根到茎到叶，诅咒他们至永恒地狱。"劳伦斯希望其他作家能站出来，面对法庭对《虹》的压制进行公开抗议："我觉得要是像班尼特那些作家能公开抗议就好了。约翰·德林瓦特刚才来了，他急切地想做点什么。很多人对这件事都义愤填膺。要不您组织一个公开抗议活动，怎么样？这样再好不过了。"

Fig.2

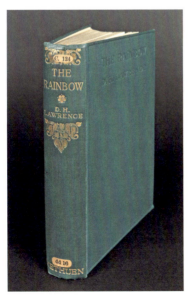

The Rainbow by D.H. Lawrence (London: Methuen & Co., 1915), British Library C.124.dd.16.

小说《虹》的英文原版，D.H. 劳伦斯著（伦敦：梅休因出版社，1915 年）。大英图书馆藏：C.124.dd.16.

The Rainbow was not the first nor was it the last of Lawrence's works to face censorship. **[Fig. 2]** *Sons and Lovers*, his novel of 1913, had been heavily edited and was banned from public libraries. Perhaps Lawrence's most famous work, *Lady Chatterley's Lover*, written in 1928, was also banned and not published in the United Kingdom until 1960.

James Brand Pinker was a literary agent who represented numerous authors including H.G. Wells, James Joyce, Henry James and John Galsworthy.

This volume of letters was purchased by the British Library in 1998 from the bookseller R.A. Gekoski.

《虹》并不是劳伦斯第一部遭到审查的小说，也不是最后一部（图 2）。他于 1913 年出版的小说《儿子与情人》曾被大幅改动，各大公共图书馆都不予收藏。写于 1928 年的《查泰莱夫人的情人》或许是劳伦斯最著名的小说了，该书也被列为禁书，直到 1960 年才得以在英国出版发行。

詹姆斯·布兰德·平克是一位出版代理人，他代理过很多作家，其中有赫伯特·乔治·威尔斯、詹姆斯·乔伊斯、亨利·詹姆斯和约翰·高尔斯华绥。

这一宗信函由大英图书馆于 1998 年从书商 R.A. 杰寇斯基处购得。

---

1 & 2　Moore, Harry T., *The collected letters of D.H. Lawrence* (Heinemann, 1962) p. 376. This letter is not included in Add MS 74258.（哈里·T. 摩尔：《D.H. 劳伦斯书信集》(伦敦：海涅曼出版公司，1962 年）第 376 页。这封信并没有包含在藏品 Add MS 74258 之中。）

3　Add MS 74258 ff. 22–23. 18 November 1915.（见于藏品编号 Add MS 74258 ff. 22–23. 的劳伦斯亲笔信，信的日期为 1915 年 11 月 18 日。）

劳伦斯作品在中国
David Herbert Lawrence's works in China

　　由于劳伦斯在其作品中激烈批判了当时的英国社会与现代工业文明，敢于积极肯定、直率表现性爱等人性中原始、"肉体性"的一面，他生前在英国文坛毁誉参半。直到20世纪中叶，随着英美社会的变革，以1960年《查泰莱夫人的情人》全本终于在英国合法出版等事件为标志，劳伦斯作为20世纪英国文学重要代表人物的地位终于得以奠定。劳伦斯作品在中国的译介、研究在将近一个世纪间同样经历了曲折的历程。

作品译介
Translations

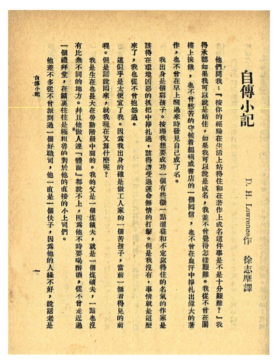

《自传小记》，徐志摩译，《新月》第三卷第四期，1930 年。
'Autobiographical Sketch', trans. by Xu Zhimo, *Xin Yue* (*Crescent Moon*), Vol. 3, No. 4, 1930.

中文世界目前所知最早发表的劳伦斯作品译文是徐志摩翻译的散文《说"是一个男子"》，刊载于 1925 年《晨报副刊·文学旬刊》第七十二期。此后徐志摩又翻译了劳伦斯的《性对爱》《自传小记》等文章。在《自传小记》中，劳伦斯详细讲述了自己的家庭背景、早年经历和走上文学道路的经过，认为当时英国社会森严的阶级界限"造成一个渊谷，一种隔绝，最好的人情的流通丧失在这上面"，鲜明表示了自己的态度，"我不能把我从我自己的阶级转移到中等阶级。我无论如何也不能放弃我的热情的意识和我与我的同类与牲畜与地土间的深厚的血液的关联"。

《二十岁的女子》，谢保康译，《狮吼》复刊第七期，1928 年。

'Laura Philippine', trans. by Xie Baokang, *Shi Hou* (*Lions' Roars*), No. 7, 1928.

1928 年，《狮吼》月刊复刊第七期刊登了谢保康翻译的劳伦斯《二十岁的女子》，篇末有"译者附注"："本篇原名 Laura Philippine，刊本年七月七日 T. P. 周刊。篇中人名，因字义上有关系，故未译音。"事实上译文中不仅人名、地名大多保留原文，就连"Cocktail"（鸡尾酒）、"Charleston"（查尔斯顿舞）、"Jazz"（爵士舞）等普通名词都未译出。

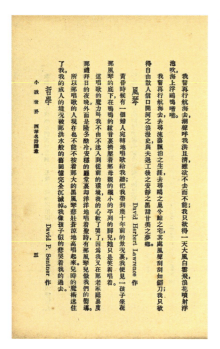

《西洋名诗译意：风琴》，苏兆龙译，《小说世界》附刊《民众文学》第十八卷第四期，1929 年。
'Piano', trans. by Su Zhaolong, *Xiao Shuo Shi Jie* (*Fiction World*)，Vol. 18，No. 4，1929.

《二青鸟》，杜衡译，水沫书店，1929 年。
Two Blue Birds and Other Stories，trans. by Du Heng，Shui Mo Book Company，1929.

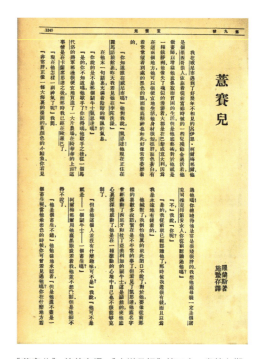

《薏赛儿》，施蛰存译，《小说月报》第二十一卷第九期，1930 年。
'None of That', trans. by Shi Zhecun，*The Short Story Magazine*，Vol. 21，No. 9，1930.

1929 年，商务印书馆出版的《小说世界》杂志附刊《民众文学》第十八卷第四期发表苏兆龙译《西洋名诗译意》，其中包括了劳伦斯的《风琴》，这是现在所知最早的劳伦斯诗歌汉译。

1929 年，上海水沫书店出版了杜衡翻译的《二青鸟》，收录了《二青鸟》(*Two Blue Birds*)、《爱岛的人》(*The Man Who Loved Islands*)、《病了的煤矿夫》(*A Sick Collier*) 三篇短篇小说。这是目前所知出版最早的劳伦斯作品汉译单行本。杜衡的译文在字词、句法等方面都尽量贴近原文，显得颇为"欧化"。译序简要介绍了劳伦斯的生平和创作特点，认为他的诗"充满着一种景色的美与原质的爱底赏鉴"，小说"描绘爱欲而带一种玩世派的情调，遂为英国现代一大作家"。

1930 年劳伦斯逝世后，《小说月报》除了发表杜衡的纪念文章之外，还刊载了著名作家施蛰存翻译的短篇小说《薏赛儿》(*None of That*)。施蛰存在后记中说明由于小说原题"意义含有双关，不易移译"，因此译文改用小说女主人公薏赛儿（Ethel）命名。

《樱草的路》，唐锡如译，《文艺月刊》第四卷第四期，1933 年。
'The Primrose Path', trans. by Tang Xiru, *Literature and Arts Monthly*, Vol. 4, No. 4, 1933.

《女店主》，唐锡如译，《新文学》第一卷第二号，1935 年。
'Samson and Delilah', trans. by Tang Xiru, *New Literature*, Vol. 1, No. 2, 1933.

　　1933 年，唐锡如翻译了劳伦斯的短篇小说《樱草的路》，发表于《文艺月刊》第四卷第四期。小说标题典出莎士比亚《哈姆雷特》，指放纵逸乐、通向毁灭之路。1935 年，唐锡如还翻译了《女店主》，发表于《新文学》一卷二号。小说原题借用了《圣经》中参孙与大利拉的典故，暗示了主角南侃维斯太太和出走多年后突然回家的丈夫威廉之间爱恨交织的复杂关系。《樱草的路》在这一时期还有丁斐如的译文，1938 年刊载于《沙漠画报》。

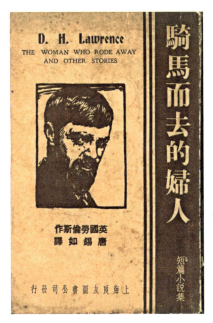

《骑马而去的妇人》，唐锡如译，上海良友图
书公司，1936 年。
*The Woman Who Rode Away and Other
Stories*，trans. by Tang Xiru, Shanghai
Companion Book Company, 1936.

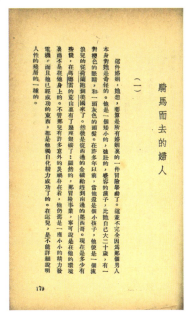

　　1936 年，上海良友图书公司出版了唐锡如翻译的《骑马而去的妇人》，收录了《女店主》、
《樱草的路》、《芳妮与安妮》(*Fanny and Annie*)、《微笑》(*Smile*)、《太阳》(*Sun*)、《冬天的孔
雀》(*Wintry Peacock*)、《骑马而去的妇人》(*The Woman Who Rode Away*) 七篇中短篇小说。

《热恋》，钱歌川译，中华书局，1935 年。
In Love and Other Stories, trans. by Qian Gechuan, Zhonghua Book Company, 1935.

　　1935 年，钱歌川翻译的《热恋》由中华书局出版，包括了俄（苏）(左琴科、谢尔盖·谢苗诺夫)、英（高尔斯华绥、劳伦斯、阿道司·赫胥黎等）、美（辛克莱·刘易斯、马克·吐温、爱德加·爱伦·坡、舍伍德·安德森等）、匈牙利（米克沙特）等国 14 位作家的 14 篇短篇小说，而以劳伦斯《热恋》一篇作为书名，封面、版权页等处所列作者也只有劳伦斯一人，可见劳伦斯在译者、读者心目中的地位已相当重要。

20世纪30年代，还陆续有不少劳伦斯作品的译文发表，如逸翔译《英国，我的英国》、陈梦家译《两只青鸟》《一个绝望的女人》、尔流译《男性与孔雀》、李慧娟译《热恋》、刘强译《蓝皮鞋》、于佑虞译《落花生》，等等。

《劳伦斯的人生与恋爱观》，赵简子译，《万人月报》1931年第二期。
'Men, Women, Life and Love', trans. by Zhao Jianzi, *Millions' Monthly*, No. 2, 1931.

《英国，我的英国》，逸翔译，《南大半月刊》1933年第三/四期。
'England, My England', trans. by Yi Xiang, *Nan Kai University Fortnightly*, Nos. 3-4, 1933.

《两只青鸟》，陈梦家译，《文艺月刊》第六卷第四期，1934年。
'Two Blue Birds', trans. by Chen Mengjia, *Literature and Arts Monthly*, Vol. 6, No. 4, 1934.

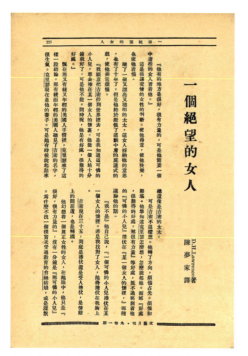

《一个绝望的女人》，陈梦家译，《文艺月刊》
第九卷第一期，1936 年。
'Jimmy and the Desperate Woman',
trans. by Chen Mengjia, *Literature and
Arts Monthly*, Vol. 9, No. 1, 1936.

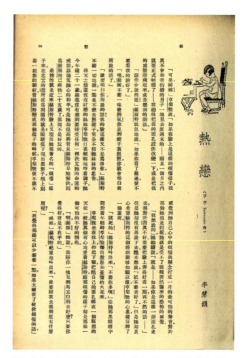

《热恋》，李慧娟译，《新中华》第三卷第十七期，
1935 年。
'In Love', trans. by Li Hui Juan, *Xin Zhonghua*
(*New China*), Vol. 3, No. 17, 1935.

《蓝皮鞋》，刘强译，《青
年学术研究会季刊》第
一卷第二期，1935 年。
'The Blue Moccasins',
trans. by Liu Qiang,
*Quaterly of the Youth's
Academic Research
Society*, Vol. 1, No. 2,
1935.

《劳伦斯书信二篇》，柳川译，《绿洲》第一卷
第二期，1936 年。
'Two Letters by D.H. Lawrence：I. To
Edward Gamett; II. To Ernest Collins',
trans. by Liu Chuan, *Lü Zhou*（*Oasis*），
Vol. 1, No. 2, 1936.

《印第安部落的舞蹈者：［画图］》,《文学》
第五卷第一期，1935 年。
'Pueblo Indian Dancers'，（Painting, Circa
1925，pen & ink on paper），*Literature*，
Vol. 5, No. 1, 1935.

    值得一提的是，此时劳伦斯的书信也已经有汉译问世，如柳川译《劳伦斯书信二篇》（《绿
洲》第一卷第二期，1936）等。就连劳伦斯的绘画也已经有所介绍，如 1935 年《文学》第五
卷第一期就登载了劳伦斯的画作《印第安部落的舞蹈者》。

《契脱来夫人的情人》，T.N.T. 译，《约翰声》第四十六卷，1935 年。
Lady Chatterley's Lover（*Excerpts*），trans. by 'T.N.T.', *St. John's Echo*, Vol. 46, 1935.

《贾泰来夫人之恋人》，王孔嘉译，《天地人》创刊号，1936 年。
Lady Chatterley's Lover（*Chapter I-IX*），trans. by Wang Kongjia, fortnightly serial in *Tian Di Ren*（*Heaven，Earth and Men*），1936.

　　《查泰莱夫人的情人》是劳伦斯后期的代表作，也是他生前身后引发争议最大的作品之一。从 1928 年出版到 20 世纪 40 年代，这部小说在中国受到了特别的重视，介绍、评论颇为集中。1935 年，《约翰声》杂志发表了署名"T.N.T."翻译的女主角与情人暂别一段，题名《契脱来夫人的情人》。1936 年，徐讦、孙成主编的《天地人》杂志刊载了王孔嘉翻译的《贾泰来夫人之恋人》前九章。

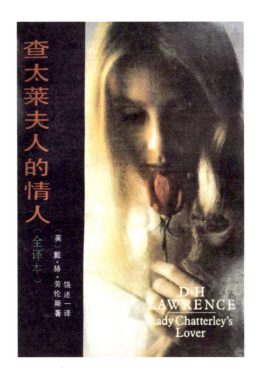

《查太莱夫人的情人》，饶述一译，湖南人民出版社，1986年。
Lady Chatterley's Lover, trans. by Rao Shuyi, reprinted by Hunan People's Publishing House, 1986.

　　1936年，饶述一翻译的《查太莱夫人的情人》由译者以个人名义出版，这是这部小说的第一个全译本。译本水平颇高，对原文的理解、译文文字的表达相当准确流畅。饶述一在译本序中高度肯定了这部小说的思想意义和艺术成就，明确指出劳伦斯的理想在于破除世俗社会对于性爱问题的神秘看法，"脱离所有过去的种种愚民的禁忌，从我们人身所最需要，最深刻地需要的起点，用伟大的温情的接触，去产生新道德，新社会，新生命"。尽管只印行了2000册，这一译本却在抗战时期的大后方与沦陷区广为流传，出现了大量盗版本。1949年后又在港台地区出现多种翻印本、改编本，成为流行读物。在中国内地，此书虽多年未能再版，却以手抄本等形式私下流传。1986年，湖南人民出版社根据1936年原版重版此书，却又因种种原因遭禁。这一译本在半个世纪中的命运沉浮可谓劳伦斯作品在中国曲折传播史的缩影。毋庸讳言，《查太莱夫人的情人》的"声名远播"在一定程度上也使得大众读者对此书乃至劳伦斯整体形象的认识产生了一些偏差。[1] 对于译者"饶述一"的真实身份，学界虽有不少猜测，却至今未有定论。

1　例如即使是朱天文、侯孝贤等编剧，陈坤厚导演的台湾"新电影"代表作《小毕的故事》（1983）中，都以小毕房中私藏《查泰莱夫人的情人》来暗示"青春期萌动"。

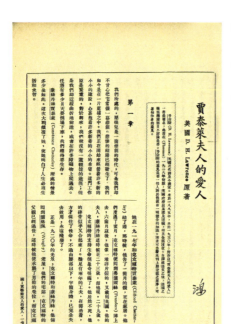

《贾泰莱夫人的爱人》，"鸿"译，《光华附中半月刊》第五卷第三／四期，1937年。

Lady Chatterley's Lover (Excerpts), trans. by 'Hong', *Fortnightly Magazine of the High School Attached to Kwang Hua University*, Vol. 5, 1937.

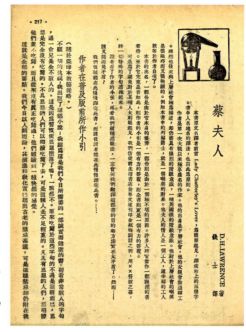

《蔡夫人》，钱士译，《大众》1943年第1期。

Lady Chatterley's Lover (Excerpts), trans. by Qian Shi, *Da Zhong* (*The Mass*), No. 1, 1943.

在饶述一译本出版后，还出现了署名"鸿"译《贾泰莱夫人的爱人》(《光华附中半月刊》1937年)、钱士译《蔡夫人》(《大众》，1943年)等部分章节的译文。

20世纪40年代，劳伦斯作品的译介仍在继续。如1942年《诗创作》杂志发表的邹绿芷译《现代英国诗抄》中包括了劳伦斯的诗歌名篇《蛇》；同年，北平出版的《吾友》杂志第二卷七至十二期连载发表了岳蓬翻译的短篇小说《蔷薇园里的影子》。此外还有花神译《恩与爱》、王还译《美妇人》《爱岛屿的人》、蒋炳贤译《鸟的啸歌》等，《美妇人》后来还被收入柳无忌编《世界短篇小说精华》。

《现代英国诗抄：蛇》，邹绿芷译，《诗创作》第十七期，1942年。
'Snake', trans. by Zou Lü zhi, *Shi Chuang Zuo* (*Poetical Composition*), No. 17, 1942.

《蔷薇园里的影子》，岳蓬译，《吾友》第二卷第七至十二期，1942年。
'The Shadow in the Rose Garden', trans. by Yue Peng, *Wu You* (*My Friends*), Vol. 2, Nos. 7-12, 1942.

《美妇人》，王还译，《时与潮文艺》第三卷第二期，1944 年。

'The Lovely Lady', trans. by Wang Huan, *Shi Yu Chao Wen Yi* (*Literature and Arts of the Age and the Current*), Vol. 3, No. 2, 1944.

《鸟的啸歌》，蒋炳贤译，《时与潮文艺》第四卷第一期，1944 年。

'Whistling of Birds', trans. by Jiang Bingxian, *Shi Yu Chao Wen Yi* (*Literature and Arts of the Age and the Current*), Vol. 4, No. 1, 1944.

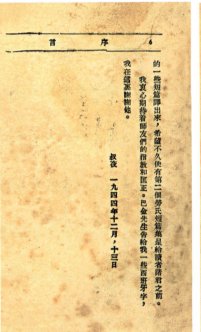

譯者序言

「騎馬而去的婦人」在桂林剛出版，發往各處的書還沒有十分之一二，桂林便下了疏散令，當時不及搶運出來，隨着便在砲火中化成灰燼。我有慈恐失掉兒子的哀痛！到重慶後，趁着失業空閒加譯了兩篇交誼文社印行，便成了現在這本「在愛情中」。

勞倫斯的文筆是非常清麗的，連最反對他的福克斯也曾這樣讚頌。他熱烈的信仰以愛爲上帝，他的小說皆以愛慾其主要動力而得到表現。他對於藝術的認真和心理分析的仔細有着登峰造極的成就，由此也可以看出他在英國文壇地位之高和讚者之衆。他的作品很多，但介紹到中國來的卻沒有多少，我很想先將勞氏的一些短篇譯出來，希望不久他有第二個勞氏短篇集呈給讀者諸君之前。我衷心期待着師友們的指教和匡正。巴金先生告給我一些西班牙字，我在這裏謝謝他。

叔夜 一九四四年十二月，十三日

《在爱情中》，叔夜译，文学编译出版公司，1946 年 3 月沪一版。
In Love and Other Two Stories, trans. by Shu Ye, Literature Translation Publishing Company（Shanghai），1946.

　　1944 年，叔夜译《骑马而去的妇人》由桂林春潮社出版，但不久之后就大部分毁于战火。译者到重庆后又加译了《微笑》《在爱情中》两篇，由说文社出版。1946 年又由上海文学编译出版公司以《在爱情中》之名重新出版。译序中简要概括了劳伦斯作品的主题、风格，认为"劳伦斯的文笔是非常清丽的"，"他的小说皆以爱欲为其主要动力而得到表现"，"对于艺术的认真和心理分析的仔细有着登峰造极的成就"；但也有不够确切之处，如称劳伦斯逝世后"英国国民排了数十里长的队伍参加葬仪"，就和史实大相径庭。[1]

1　1930 年劳伦斯病逝后，仅有十位亲友参加了简单的葬礼。1935 年，根据劳伦斯夫人弗丽达的愿望，劳伦斯的骨灰最终安放于他生前与弗丽达在美国新墨西哥州陶斯县购置的牧场内的纪念堂中。1956 年弗丽达去世，安于纪念堂外。她在遗嘱中将牧场捐赠给新墨西哥大学，作为劳伦斯纪念地，今名"D.H. 劳伦斯牧场"（D.H. Lawrence Ranch）。

《木马冠军》，周易译，《译林：外国文学丛刊》1980 年 1 期。
'The Rocking-Horse Winner', trans. by Zhou Yi, *Yi Lin*, No. 1, 1980.

《劳伦斯短篇小说集》，主万译，上海译文出版社，1983 年。
Short Stories of D.H. Lawrence, trans. by Zhu Wan, Shanghai Translation Publishing House，1983.

　　20 世纪五六十年代，劳伦斯在西方文学界开始得到重新评价，声誉、影响与日俱增。然而在同时期的中国内地，他却被当作"颓废作家"简单否定，译介、研究几乎完全中断。直到改革开放之后，劳伦斯的作品才又一次出现在中国读者的视野中。1980 年的《译林》第 1 期刊登了周易翻译的短篇小说《木马冠军》(*The Rocking-Horse Winner*)，这是时隔多年后在中国内地正式发表的第一篇劳伦斯作品译文。此后劳伦斯的作品开始在外国文学刊物上陆续出现。从 20 世纪 80 年代中期开始，中国出版界出现了"劳伦斯热"，短短十余年间，劳伦斯的绝大部分作品都已翻译出版，不少代表作出现了多种译本，还有数种多卷本文集问世，成为在中国被译介最多的英国作家之一。

Sons and Lovers 的若干译本
Several translations of *Sons and Lovers*

 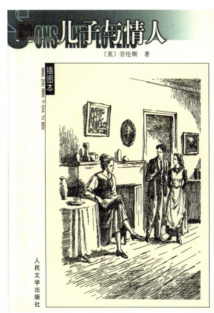 

《儿子与情人》，李健、何善强、李
晓和译，四川人民出版社，1986 年。
Trans. by Li Jian, He Shanqiang
and Li Xiaohe, Sichuan People's
Publishing House, 1986.

《儿子与情人》，陈良廷、刘文澜
译，人民文学出版社，1987 年。
Trans. by Chen Liangting and
Liu Wenlan, People's Literature
Publishing House, 2006.

《儿子与情人》，张禹九译，上海译
文出版社，2007 年。
Trans. by Zhang Yujiu, Shanghai
Translation Publishing House,
2007.

The Rainbow 的若干译本

Several Translations of *The Rainbow*

《虹落浑尘》，毕冰宾、石磊译，漓江出版社，
1992 年。
Trans. by Bi Bingbin and Shi Lei, Lijiang
Press，1992.

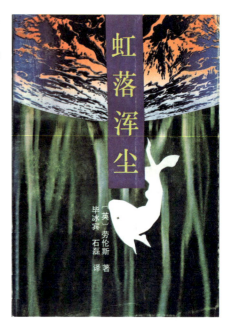

《虹》，雪崖译，云南人民出版社，1988 年。
Trans. by Xue Ya, Yunnan People's
Publishing House, 1988.

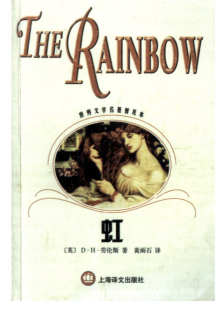

《虹》，黄雨石译，上海译文出版社，2004 年。
Trans. by Huang Yushi, Shanghai Translation
Publishing House，2004.

Women in Love 的若干译本

Several translations of *Women in Love*

《恋爱中的妇女》，梁一三译，中国文联
出版公司，1987 年。
Trans. by Liang Yisan, The Publishing
Company of Federation of Literature &
Art of China, 1987.

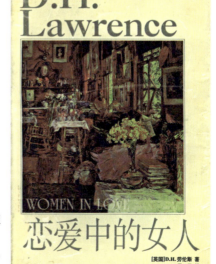

《恋爱中的女人》，黑马译，译林出版
社，1999 年。
Trans. by Hei Ma, Yilin Press,
1999.

Lady Chatterley's Lover 的若干译本

Several translations of *Lady Chatterley's Lover*

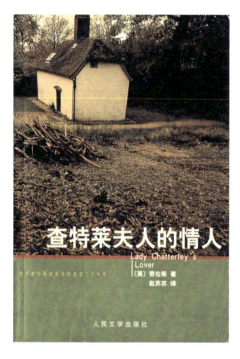

《查特莱夫人的情人》，赵苏苏译，人民文学出版社，1994 年。
Trans. by Zhao Susu, People's Literature Publishing House，1994.

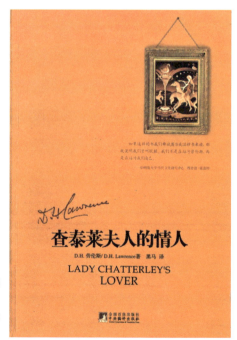

《查泰莱夫人的情人》，黑马译，中央编译出版社，2010 年。
Trans. by Hei Ma, Central Compilation & Translation Press, 2010.

《影朦胧：劳伦斯诗选 》，黄锡祥译，
花城出版社，1990 年。
*Shadows：Selected Poems of D.H.
Lawrence*，trans. by Huang Xixiang，
Huacheng Press，1990.

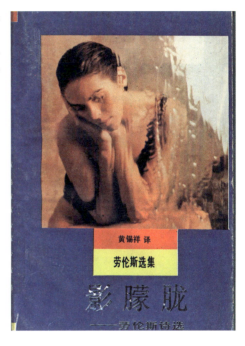

《劳伦斯诗选 》，吴笛译，漓江出版社，1995 年。
Selected Poems of D.H. Lawrence，trans. by
Wu Di, Lijiang Press，1995.

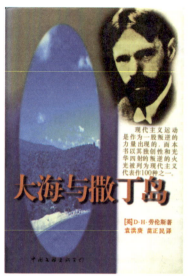

《大海与撒丁岛》，袁洪庚、苗正民译，中国文联出版公司，1997 年。
Sea and Sardinia，trans. by Yuan Honggeng and Miao Zhengmin，The Publishing Company of Federation of Literature & Art of China，1997.

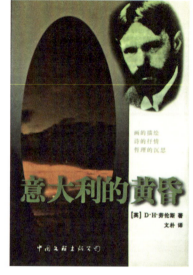

《意大利的黄昏》，文朴译，中国文联出版公司，1997 年。
Twilight in Italy，trans. by Wen Pu，The Publishing Company of Federation of Literature & Art of China，1997.

《劳伦斯文集》，北方文艺出版社，1999 年。
Collected Works of D.H. Lawrence，The North Literature & Art Publishing House，1999.

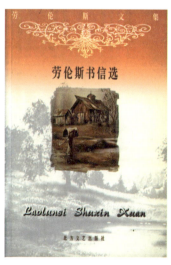

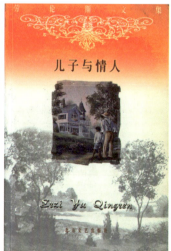

《D.H. 劳伦斯长篇小说全集》(12 卷)，山东文艺出版社，2010 年。
Complete Novels of D.H. Lawrence (12 vols.), Shandong Literature and Art Publishing House, 2010.

《劳伦斯文集》(10 卷)，人民文学出版社，2014 年。
Collected Works of D.H. Lawrence (10 vols.), People's Literature Publishing House，2014.

评论研究

Reviews

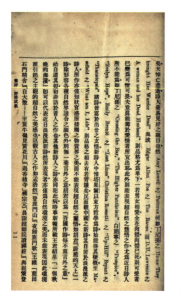
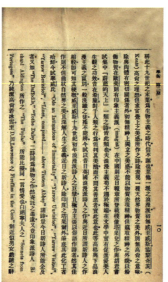

胡先骕《书评：评尝试集》，《学衡》1922 年第 2 期。
Hu Xiansu's negative remarks on 'Fireflies in the Corn' and 'A Woman and Her Dead Husband' by D.H. Lawarence in 'On Hu Shi's *Chang Shi Ji（Poetical Experiments）*', *Critical Review*, No. 2, 1922.

　　目前所知中文世界最早论及劳伦斯作品的文章是著名植物学家、诗人、评论家、"学衡派"代表人物胡先骕的《评尝试集》，胡先骕出于中国传统文学立场与乃师白璧德的"新人文主义"思想，在此文中对胡适《尝试集》以至整个新诗运动都持否定态度。文章第六节《古学派浪漫派之艺术观及其优劣》提及了劳伦斯的两首诗，认为"Fireflies in the Corn""近似男女戏谑之辞"，"A Woman and Her Dead Husband""品格尤为卑下"，"岂真宜笃于爱情者所宜出耶"，无法与白朗宁夫人（Elizabeth Barrett Browning）、丁尼孙（Alfred Tennyson）、波（埃德加·爱伦·坡，Edgar Allan Poe）等 19 世纪诗人相比。从中不难看出他对英美文学的看法仍然囿于维多利亚时代以来的成规陈见，对劳伦斯的思想、艺术缺乏同情和理解。

郑振铎《文学大纲》第四十二章《新世纪的文学》,《小说月报》第十八卷第一期,1927年。
The Outline of Literature by Zheng Zhenduo, Chapter 42 'Literature of the New Century', *The Short Story Magazine*, Vol. 18, No. 1, 1927.

　　1927 年,郑振铎在《小说月报》连载发表《文学大纲》,第四十二章《新世纪的文学》中简单提及了"罗连斯"(劳伦斯),列举了《白孔雀》《儿子与情人》《虹》等小说书名,认为"他最近的小说《阿龙的杖》(*Aaron's Rod*)显着思想与风格的长足的进步"。

斐耶《英国新进的小说作家》，《晨报副刊》
1928 年 3 月 19～21 日。
'New Novelists in Britain' by Fei Ye, *Chen Bao Fu Kan*, Mar. 19–21, 1928.

　　1928 年 3 月，《晨报副刊》发表斐耶《英国新进的小说作家》，文中概括了劳伦斯的创作特色与文学地位。

赵景深《现代文坛杂话：罗兰斯的两性描写》，《小说月报》第十九卷第九期，1928 年。
'The Erotic Descriptions of D.H. Lawrence' by Zhao Jingshen, *The Short Story Magazine*, Vol. 19, No. 9, 1928.

赵景深《二十年来的英国小说》，《小说月报》第二十卷第八期，1929 年。
Remarks on D.H. Lawrence in 'The British Fiction of the Last Twenty Years' by Zhao Jingshen, *The Short Story Magazine*, Vol. 20, No. 8, 1929.

　　1928 年，赵景深在《小说月报・现代文坛杂话》栏目发表简讯《罗兰斯的两性描写》，报道了小说集《骑马而去的妇人》出版的消息，引用《纽约时报》评论，认为其中"以《双蓝鸟》《微笑》《恋爱了》三篇为最佳"，扼要介绍了《双蓝鸟》一篇的内容。1929 年，赵景深又先后在这一栏目中介绍了劳伦斯翻译的魏尔嘉"《露士替加那》"（*Cavalleria Rusticana*，今译《乡村骑士》[1]）出版、劳伦斯旅居佛罗伦萨、"《沙脱莱夫人的恋人们》"问世等消息。在同年发表的《二十年来英国小说》一文中，赵景深将劳伦斯列为"两性小说家"之首，简要评述了《白孔雀》、《犯罪者》（*The Trespasser*）、《儿子与爱人》、《虹》、《失去的女郎》（*The Lost Girl*）、《恋爱着的女人》、《阿郎的威权》（*Aaron's Rod*）等长篇小说。

1　意大利作曲家马斯卡尼（Pietro Mascagni, 1863 ～ 1945，赵景深文中译作"马斯开格礼"）曾根据这篇小说创作了同名歌剧《乡村骑士》(1890)，成为意大利"真实主义"歌剧最杰出的代表作，至今仍是世界歌剧舞台上久演不衰的经典剧目。

赵景深《现代文坛杂话：英国小说家罗兰斯逝世》，《小说月报》第二十一卷第四期，1930 年。

'The English Novelist D.H. Lawrence Was Dead' by Zhao Jingshen, *The Short Story Magazine*, Vol. 21, No. 4, 1930.

杜衡《罗兰斯》，《小说月报》第二十一卷第九期，1930 年。
'D.H. Lawrence' by Du Heng, *The Short Story Magazine*, Vol. 21, No. 9, 1930.

偶然《英国小说家劳伦斯逝世》，《申报》1930 年 6 月 12 日《艺术界》专栏。
'The English Novelist D.H. Lawrence Was Dead' by Wang Tiran, *The Shun Pao*, June 12, 1930.

羅蘭斯逝世

楊昌溪

——最近逝世的英國小說家——

英國自來傳統的瞽氣很重，所以在過去的文人如雪萊和拜倫都含愁的逃往意大利。而且關於性方面描寫的作家的作品是不能享着好運道，似乎比關於政治的抨擊還要難於受寬容。在近代以描寫兩性關係聞名的小說家羅蘭斯（D,H.Lawrence）是比任何人都難於在本國居留，意大利宛如古今文人遁跡休養的唯一場所，他從本國間接受了刺激而便住在意大利佛羅稜薩的略普里。(Oreo'i) 在今年三月他竟在那兒長逝了。

當他初在英國文壇上露頭角的時候，許多人謠傳他的生命不久便要為肺癆所挫折。因此，在關心他的人一讀到第一部小說白孔雀 (The white Peacock) 時便四處的訪問

杨昌溪《罗兰斯逝世：最近逝世的英国小说家》，《现代文学》第一卷第一期，1930 年。
'D.H. Lawrence: the Recently Deceased English Novelist' by Yang Changxi, *Modern Literature*, Vol. 1, No. 1, 1930.

羅蘭斯論

英國　華倫 (C.Henry Warren) 作

趙景深 譯

羅蘭斯（G.H.Lawrence）死了。他於上月（三月）死於布羅溫斯 (Provence)。在他死前一些年，他大半的光陰都消磨在南方——意大利，法蘭西，墨西哥——因此他的大部分的較近作品,常用各種形式，來寫太陽的照臨。他的心中異教徒的血兇猛而且熱情的適應着太陽，他似乎在這裏面看見了一種生命之途的象徵。近些年來他最熱烈的呼聲就是不滿意於現代的生活過於『反對太陽』了。在他的眼裏看來，反對太陽就等於毀滅和死亡。他在最近的一本詩集裏寫道：『良心就是感覺太陽，我們的深沈的性情就是不要反對太陽。』

他所寫的最好的短篇小說之一 (收在騎馬而去的婦人

［英］华伦《罗兰斯论》，赵景深译，《现代文学》第一卷第一期，1930 年。
'On D.H. Lawrence' by C. Henry Warren, trans. by Zhao Jingshen, *Modern Literature*, Vol. 1, No. 1, 1930.

　　1930 年 3 月 2 日劳伦斯逝世。3 月 24 日，《大公报·文学副刊》率先报道了这一消息，赵景深很快也在《小说月报》上报道了劳伦斯去世的消息。《小说月报》第二十一卷第九期还发表了杜衡的纪念文章《罗兰斯》。6 月 12 日，《申报》刊登了汪倜然《英国小说家劳伦斯逝世》一文，肯定他是"现代文坛上的一位要人，英国寥寥可数的几个近代重要作家之一"，特别强调了他"身体中的异教徒的血"、重视人性中"肉的方面""厌弃一切的优美"而追求"男性的"风格等思想特征和艺术特点。7 月，赵景深主编的《现代文学》第一卷第一期又发表杨昌溪《罗兰斯逝世：最近逝世的英国小说家》，较为详细地介绍了劳伦斯的生平、思想和创作。同期还发表了赵景深翻译的 C.H. 华伦的《罗兰斯论》。甚至一向以文化保守主义立场著称的《学衡》杂志都刊登了劳伦斯照片以示纪念，标志着劳伦斯的文学成就已经得到中国文化界的公认。

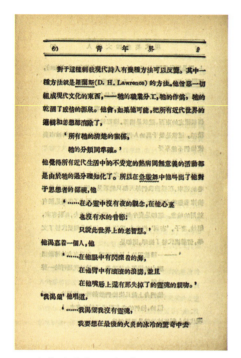

温源宁《现代英美四大诗人》，顾绥昌译，《青年界》第二卷第二期，1932 年。
'Four Great Modern Poets of Britain and United States' by Wen Yuanning, trans.
by Gu Shouchang, *Qing Nian Jie*（*Youth World*）, Vol. 2, No. 2, 1932.

南星《谈劳伦斯的诗》,《文饭小品》
1935 年第 5 期。
'On D.H. Lawrence's Poems' by
Nan Xing, *Wen Fan Xiao Pin*, No. 5,
1935.

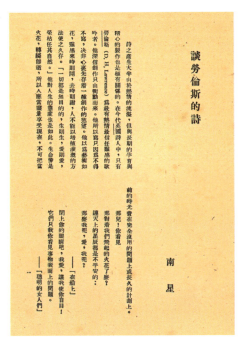

20 世纪 30 年代，中国文学界对劳伦斯的诗歌也有了更为公允深刻的评价。1932 年 9 月，上海《青年界》杂志刊登了时任北京大学英文系主任、著名文学评论家温源宁的文章《现代英美四大诗人》(原为此年 5 月 8 日在北平万国美术研究所的演讲)。此文将劳伦斯与德勒迈尔（Walter de la Mare）、圣得堡格（Carl Sandburg，今译卡尔·桑德堡）、哀里奥德（T.S. 艾略特）相提并论，认为他们的诗作以不同的方法表现了对于现代机械文明下人性异化的反抗，而劳伦斯的反抗方法就是彻底否定现代文化，"回到本能的生活中去"。1935 年，诗人南星在《文饭小品》杂志发表了自己翻译的《病》等劳伦斯诗作和评论《谈劳伦斯的诗》，分析了劳伦斯诗歌的思想内容、艺术特色，是目前所知中文世界第一篇劳伦斯诗歌专论。

邵洵美：《金屋谈话（二）：一本赤裸裸的小说》，《狮吼》复刊第九期，1928 年。
'Remarks from the Golden House：II. A Naked Novel' by Shao Xunmei, *Shi Hou*（*Lions' Roars*）, No. 9, 1928.

李辰冬《法译贾泰蓝夫人的情夫及其辩护》，《新月》第四卷第六期，1933 年。
'The French Version of *Lady Chatterley's Lover* and a Defence of This Novel' by Li Chendong, *Xin Yue*（*Crescent Moon*）, Vol. 4, No. 6, 1933.

郁达夫《读劳伦斯的小说》，《人间世》第十四期，1934 年。
'Reading D.H. Lawrence's Novel' by Yu Dafu, *Ren Jian Shi*, No. 14, 1934.

林语堂《谈劳伦斯》,《人间世》第十九
期, 1935 年
'On D.H. Lawrence' by Lin Yutang,
Ren Jian Shi, No. 19, 1935.

邵洵美《读劳伦斯的小说》,《人言周刊》第一卷第
三十八期, 1934 年。
'Reading D.H. Lawrence's Novel: A Letter in
Response to Mr Yu Dafu' by Shao Xunmei, *Ren
Yan Weekly*, Vol. 1, No. 38, 1934.

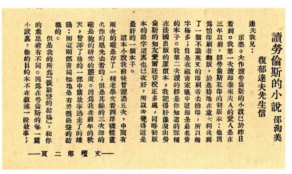

　　1928 年,《查泰莱夫人的情人》在意大利出版。著名诗人、出版家邵洵美主编的《狮吼》
杂志复刊第九期《金屋谈话》栏目第二节《一本赤裸裸的小说》迅即报道了这一消息,认为
此书"句句是力的描写与表现,使读者的心,从头到底被他擒捉住"。1933 年,《新月》杂志
《海外出版界》栏目发表了李辰冬的文章《法译贾泰蓝夫人的情夫及其辩护》,将劳伦斯的这部
小说与《金瓶梅》相比较,认为"二者都系自然主义的作品,而且都持肉灵一致的精神",但
"以彻底的,有思想的而论,当以《贾泰蓝夫人的情夫》为佳",详细分析了小说中的克里福爵
士、康司当斯、莫鲁(Oliver Mellors)等主要人物形象和情节主线,指出劳伦斯的用意在于批
判英国社会与现代文明,主张彻底改革,结论虽然遗憾于劳伦斯"太注重了表现他的思想,他
的人生观",以致人物描写不够生动,但依然肯定"这是一部古今来稀世的珍品,是现代青年
男女的正当读物"。在当时此书在各国都饱受攻击污蔑的时代背景下,这样的高度评价可谓不
同凡响。此后郁达夫、邵洵美、林语堂、章益等著名作家、学者也陆续发表文章,对劳伦斯的
这部小说给予了中肯的评价。

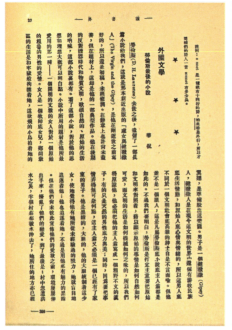

华侃《外国文学：劳伦斯最后的小说》，《世界杂志》第一卷第二期，1931 年。
'D.H. Lawrence's Last Novel' by Hua Kan, *World Magazine*, Vol. 1, No. 2, 1931.

孙晋三《现代文艺作家介绍：劳伦斯》，《清华周刊》第四十二卷第九／十期，1934 年。
'Introduction to Modern Writers：D.H. Lawrence' by Sun Jinsan, *Tsing Hua Weekly*, Vol. 42, Nos. 9–10, 1934.

丽尼《劳伦斯的书简》，《文学》第五卷第一期，1935 年。
'Book Review：*Letters of D.H. Lawrence*' by Li Ni, *Literature*, Vol. 5, No. 1, 1935.

未庄《劳伦斯的"默示录"》，《清华周刊》第
四十二卷第三／四期，1934 年。
'D.H. Lawrence's *Apocalypse*' by Wei Zhuang,
Tsing Hua Weekly, Vol. 42, Nos. 3–4, 1934.

V.S. Pritchett《劳伦斯研究》，华蒂译，《人间》第一
卷第四期，1946 年。
'On D.H. Lawrence' by V.S. Pritchett, trans. by
Hua Di, *Ren Jian*, Vol. 1, No. 4, 1946.

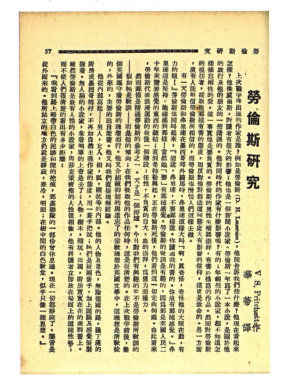

20 世纪三四十年代，对劳伦斯作品的评介文章还散见于各种报刊。

金东雷《英国文学史纲》第十二章《现代文学》第八节《劳伦斯》，商务印书馆，1937 年。

The Outline of the History of English Literature by Jin Donglei, Chapter 12 'Modern Literature' Section 8 'D.H. Lawrence', the Commercial Press, 1937.

第八節　勞倫斯

近代的盧梭——勞倫斯——有人說大衞·赫勃脫·勞倫斯(David Herbert Lawrence)(註二三)之產生於英國小說界正如盧梭(Rousseau)之產生於法國他反抗現社會的精神於此可見自從蒲洛特博士(Dr. Sigmund Freud)創造性慾說及心理分析說後英國小說界上有個勞倫斯爲之張目紳士階級一般人嫌惡他說他淫但他說他們是平民，不認識社會普通的現象並且有了智識的人無論做什麼事情總是矯揉造作，不明全體公說公有理婆說婆有理我們不替他們下什麼斷語不替勞倫斯是英國文學界上的反動人物，不我們總得承認爲了他的著作提倡着火一般的威情生活描寫着男女間熱烈的性戀愛英國政府曾屢次派人查禁幾乎處刑處徒刑後來他不能安居祖國而漫遊各處，終至天壽而他的天才、毅力和遭遇很和盧梭(Rousseau)相似假如他能長壽一切他所認爲疑難的問題將迎刃而解不幸他僅以四十五歲的年紀去世留着的著作，不能使人們加添更多的智識關於宇宙的答案始終不得而知我認爲這是人類的損失不僅勞倫斯個人的厄運而已。

勞倫斯的一生——一八八七年，勞倫斯生於娜丁漢希(Nottinghamshire)的伊司脫胡特(Eastwood)。他的父親是煤礦裏的工人每月所得薪金極微沒有力量培植兒子去受普通的教育但他的母親很能幹把勞倫斯送入娜丁漢希師範學校(Nottinghamshire Normal School)讀書又竭力替兒子謀得免費學額十六歲，他在師範學校畢業後來就當小學教師課餘遵從校長求學。二十一歲，仍得免費入職業學校當時假如沒有他母親的遠大眼光勞倫斯恐怕也去學工或做些商業他的天才將埋沒不彰所以他的成功全是母親的教導之力。

二十三歲，他到倫敦去當教師都市的現象和風氣，使他在智識方面有不少進步後來他又到克勞敦(Croy-

四六七

第十二章　現代文學

　　特别值得一提的是，1937 年出版的金东雷《英国文学史纲》一书为劳伦斯专列一节，全面评述了他的生平事迹、主要作品与思想作风，称赞他是"近代的卢梭"，"新浪漫主义者的首倡者"。

　　1981年，《世界文学》杂志发表了赵少伟《戴·赫·劳伦斯的社会批判三部曲》一文，中肯地分析了劳伦斯的代表作《虹》《恋爱中的女人》与《查泰莱夫人的情人》，认为这三部小说集中体现了劳伦斯对资本主义社会的批判，成为新时期劳伦斯研究的开山之作。自此之后，随着劳伦斯作品译介高潮的到来，对劳伦斯的评论研究也出现了"百花齐放"的繁荣局面。以传记而论，如劳伦斯夫人弗丽达的回忆录《不是我，是风》，劳伦斯生前好友理查德·奥尔丁顿[1]《一个天才的画像，但是……：D.H.劳伦斯传》，艾米丽·汉恩[2]《劳伦斯和他身边的女人们》，萨嘉《被禁止的作家：D.H.劳伦斯传》等都被翻译出版。评论著作中重要的则有蒋炳贤编《劳伦斯评论集》、蒋家国《重建人类的伊甸园：劳伦斯长篇小说研究》、刘洪涛《荒原与拯救：现代主义语境中的劳伦斯小说》等。

赵少伟《戴·赫·劳伦斯的社会批判三部曲》，《世界文学》1981年第2期。
'D.H. Lawrence's Trilogy of Social Criticism' by Zhao Shaowei, *World Literature*, No. 2, 1981.

1　理查德·奥尔丁顿（1892～1962），英国作家、诗人，以一战题材的长篇小说《英雄之死》(1929)闻名。《一个天才的画像，但是……》原著于1950年出版。
2　艾米丽·汉恩（1905～1997），中文名项美丽，美国记者、作家。1935年至1938年旅居上海，与邵洵美、宋氏姐妹等中国名人交往密切。《劳伦斯和他身边的女人们》原著于1975年出版。

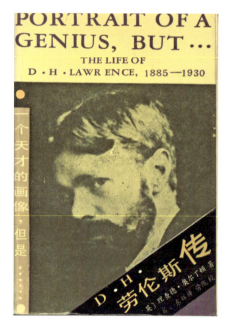

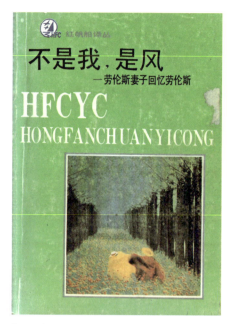

［英］理查德·奥尔丁顿《一个天才的画像，但是……：D.H. 劳伦斯传》，冰宾、东辉译，天津人民出版社，1989。

D.H. Lawrence：*Portrait of a Genius, But ...* by Richard Aldington, trans. by Bi Bingbin and Dong Hui, Tianjin People's Publishing House, 1989.

《不是我，是风——劳伦斯妻子回忆劳伦斯》，姚暨荣译，百花文艺出版社，1991 年。

'*Not I, but the Wind...*', a memoir by Frieda Lawrence, trans. by Yao Jirong, Baihua Literature and Arts Publishing House, 1991.

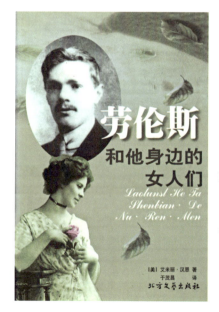

［美］艾米丽·汉恩《劳伦斯和他身边的女人们》，于茂昌译，北方文艺出版社，1998 年。

Lorenzo：*D.H. Lawrence and the Women Who Loved Him* by Emily Hahn, trans. by Yu Maochang, The North Literature and Art Literature Publishing House, 1998.

[英] 基思·萨嘉《被禁止的作家：D.H. 劳伦斯传》，王增澄译，辽宁教育出版社，1998 年。
The Life of D.H. Lawrence by Keith Sagar, trans. by Wang Zengcheng, Liaoning Education Publishing House, 1998.

《劳伦斯评论集》，蒋炳贤编，上海文艺出版社，1995 年。
D.H. Lawrence：A Collection of Critical Sources, ed. by Jiang Bingxian, Shanghai Literature and Art Publishing House, 1995.

刘洪涛《荒原与拯救：现代主义语境中的劳伦斯小说》，中国社会科学出版社，2007 年。
Waste Land and Salvation：D.H. Lawrence's Fiction in Modernist Context by Liu Hongtao, China Social Sciences Press，2007.

从欧洲到中国：劳伦斯致德国友人马克斯·摩尔书信的万里漂流

From Europe to China: the odyssey of
D.H. Lawrence's letters to Max Mohr

　　《天下月刊》是 1930 年代中国影响最大、最重要的一本由中国人主创的英文文学刊物。在 1935 年第一、第二期上，刊登了劳伦斯在 1927 至 1930 年间写给德国友人、作家马克斯·摩尔（Max Mohr，1891～1937）的 30 多封信件，内容涉及劳伦斯夫妇的旅程行迹、《查泰莱夫人的情人》创作出版过程中的种种曲折、1929 年伦敦画展风波等，对于研究劳伦斯最后几年的事迹具有相当的价值。1934 年，身为犹太人的马克斯·摩尔为躲避纳粹迫害，不得不告别妻儿，只身流亡到上海，以行医为生，1937 年淞沪战役后不久在上海去世。1935 年，马克斯·摩尔将劳伦斯写给自己的信件提供给《天下》杂志发表，并应主编温源宁之邀写了一篇简短的序言，追忆了自己当年与劳伦斯夫妇的交往点滴。

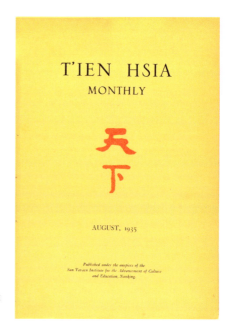

《劳伦斯致马克斯·摩尔未刊书信》，《天下月刊》第 1 卷第 1～2 期，1935 年。

'The Unpublished letters of D.H. Lawrence to Max Mohr', *T'ien Hsia Monthly*, Vol. 1, Nos.1-2, 1935.

THE UNPUBLISHED LETTERS OF D. H. LAWRENCE TO MAX MOHR
(Copyright throughout the World)

Mr. Wen Yuan-ning,
Editor-in-Chief,
T'ien Hsia Monthly.

Dear Mr. Wen,

You have asked me to write a few words by way of preface to D. H. Lawrence's letters to me. These letters speak for themselves much better than any words of mine can. Instead therefore of writing anything "literary" about them, I would rather tell you of one of the last days I spent with Lorenzo at the time he lived in the mountains with his wife Frieda near to my place in Bavaria

A little peasant-boy comes with a message from Frieda. I must go down to their house. She is standing on a wonderful blue autumn-day before the little farm-house, five minutes away from ours. She thinks that Lorenzo is going to die. She had been in his room and thought him dead already. Often before she has had this experience: again and again she had gone to his bed to see whether he was still alive or not.

Now I go into his bedroom with her. He is alive. One can see it, as his breath passes over his red beard. He opens his ice-blue eyes and smiles. He knows what we have been thinking. He gets up and we breakfast together. He laughs heartily over a story I tell him: during the preceding night I had assisted at a poor peasant-woman's delivery, and the father of the child, who was drunk, did not come back from the village-inn, in spite of the repeated urgent messages I had sent him. Lorenzo laughs heartily.

[21]

---

shop, and made "aus feinstem Rinderfett." Dass es nicht blosse Schweineschmalz ist, Gott sei Dank!

We hope to leave next Monday, 17th, for Italy. The address there is *Villa Mirenda, Scandicci, Florenz.* Greetings from us both, also to the Frau Gemahlin, and I'll tell you when to tune up the Zicharmonika.

Yours sincerely,
D. H. Lawrence.

Villa Mirenda, Scandicci,
Florence, 31st Oct. 1927.

Dear Max Mohr,

Had your letter to-day—and so you have actually sailed down the Danube on a raft! It sounds great fun: but when one comes to dead cities with exhausted people, the gilt goes off the gingerbread. But what a restless soul you are! No, you must learn to be more peaceful inside yourself, or one day you'll just explode like a rocket, and there will be nothing left but bits.

It's awfully nice of you to take so much thought and trouble for *David.** But don't you bother too much about it, you'll hate it and us in the end. I know the translation is very unsatisfactory: my sort of German, which, like your English, must go into a class by itself. And of course the whole play is too literary, too many words. The actual technique of the stage is foreign to me. But perhaps they—and you—could cut it into shape. I shall be very much surprised if they *do* play it in Berlin. The public only wants foolish realism: Hamlet in a smoking jacket.

We shall be very pleased to see you in January, wherever we are. We may be here: we may be in Cortina: or we may just possibly go to Egypt, to Cairo, where we have friends. Would you come even there? and bring the Zicharmonika to play to the pyramids? I unfortunately can't yet promise to dance—my bronchials and my cough are still a nuisance. But I want so much to be *able* to dance again. And I think if we went somewhere really amusing, I should quickly be well. My cough, like your restlessness, is a

"David," a drama by D.H.L.

[24]

The Unpublished Letters of D. H. Lawrence

good deal psychological in its origin, and a real change might cure us both. The sun shines here, but the mornings are foggy. And I no longer love Italy very much. It seems to me a stupid country. But where is one to live after all! I don't know if you would rather I wrote in my bad German—you must tell me. Tante belle cose alla Signora, anche alla figluola, e non dimentichiamo la capra.

Sincerely,
D. H. Lawrence.

Villa Mirenda, Scandicci,
Florence, 22nd Nov. 1927.

Dear Max Mohr,

A very nice and clever letter you wrote in English—suddenly your English very good! You are a man who goes by fits and starts, I believe.

When are you going to Berlin? I was thinking you might like to see my wife's sister there. I told Johanna I'd tell you.

We shan't go to Egypt—costs too much. For heaven's sake don't imagine I have got any money—I am as poor as a mouse. It is chronic with me: and shameful, really, that I make so little. Michael Arlen came in the other day—he made nearly a million dollars in America with *The Green Hat* and other things! Imagine! But he is sick, poor devil!—I think we may go to Cortina in January, to the snow: but perhaps we shall stay here, and go in April to the ranch—near Taos, near Santa Fé, in New Mexico. It's very fine there, nearly 3000 metres up, beautiful, and horses to ride. If we go, you must come too—but really. You'd love it for a while, at least. But don't mention this either, for my Schwiegermutter weeps at the very sound of the word Ranch: it is so far off.

How is the Wolfsgrube* now? Here it is warm and damp, like a hot-house: not nice. My wife is in bed with a cold: I cough,

* M.M.'s farm-house in the Bavarian Alps, near Rottach at the Tegernsee.

[25]

《劳伦斯致马克斯·摩尔未刊书信》，《天下月刊》第1卷第1～2期，1935年。
'The Unpublished letters of D.H. Lawrence to Max Mohr', *T'ien Hsia Monthly*, Vol. 1, Nos.1–2, 1935.

劳伦斯：浴火重生的作家

吴 笛

　　他如同哈代，既以丰富的小说创作赢得了巨大的声誉，又以千首诗作奠定了作为20世纪重要诗人的地位；他不同于哈代，后者是因晚年《无名的裘德》的出版遭到了社会舆论的攻击和压力而放弃小说创作，潜心写诗，在近六十岁时才出版第一本诗集，而他在一生中却同时进行诗和小说创作，并在二十几岁就出版了第一本诗集。这位比哈代迟四十五年诞生（1885），而在哈代死后两年（1930）就追随他奔赴黄泉的文学巨匠，就是 D.H. 劳伦斯。

一

　　劳伦斯是在中国最受欢迎的外国作家之一，他最主要的文学成就长篇小说和抒情诗在中国广受喜爱。他是小说领域和诗歌领域的"双料冠军"。劳伦斯的小说，尤其是他的长篇小说，所力求探索的，是人的灵魂深处的血性意识和血的领悟。他的《儿子与情人》《虹》《恋爱中的女人》《查泰莱夫人的情人》等四部最具代表性的长篇小说，具有强烈的现实主义创作风格，同时又吸纳了现代主义小说的表现手法，因而具有强烈的艺术张力，受到读者的广泛关注。

　　劳伦斯的一些长篇小说所颂扬的是和谐美满的两性关系。他关注的是人物精神和心理的发展和变化。长篇小说《儿子与情人》中，格特鲁德·科帕德常常遭遇矿工丈夫莫瑞尔的殴打，性格不合，精神追求毫不相同，在饱尝了婚姻的不幸与痛苦之后，她将本应赋予丈夫的爱全都转移到儿子的身上。而在格特鲁德·科帕德死后，她的儿子保罗感到自己的生命都随着母亲的逝去而终结，只是经过一番努力，才从这一情感的困境中摆脱出来。可见，小说所探讨的，除了精神层面的和谐，还有心理层面的"恋母情结"。

　　同样，长篇小说《虹》是一部跨越三代人的家族史，其中的女主人公厄秀拉所看重的是人的心灵，是精神层面的相互吸引，她最后抛弃的是灵肉割裂的爱情。她追求的是灵肉一致的理想的爱情，她最后终于找到了理想的彩虹。随着工业革命和人类文明对包括爱情在内的自然人性的扼杀，现实社会的和谐关系遭到了破坏，如何重新建立人与自然的和谐的关系，尤其是以性爱为代表的和谐的关系，是劳伦斯的不懈的追求，"虹"的意象便是这一和谐关系的理想象征。

同样，劳伦斯的长篇小说《恋爱中的女人》所探讨的依然是与《虹》类似的话题，这部作品以两姐妹厄秀拉和古迪兰为主人公，继续书写他们在现代社会的理想追求，描述了她们不同的情感经历，探索原始欲望与爱的激情，以及灵与肉的和谐与交融。在这部小说中，劳伦斯力图以哲学和美学的视角来书写人类的爱情。

而在长篇小说《查泰莱夫人的情人》中，劳伦斯似乎要在现代文明的废墟上重建灵肉再生的浪漫神话。尤其是女主人公康妮，嫁给青年知识分子查泰莱爵士之后不久，就与丈夫分别。查泰莱就上了前线，参加第一次世界大战。他后来在战争中负伤，由此丧失了性能力，从部队回到家乡后主要从事文学创作工作，并且思考哲学和形而上问题。于是，在康妮看来，查泰莱爵士不过是一颗纯粹思维的脑袋，而不是一个有血有肉的个体生命。她们之间的夫妻关系是残缺的。结识了守林人奥利弗·梅勒斯之后，康妮不顾梅勒斯社会地位的低下，她将她与梅勒斯的情爱，视为女性复活的体验，她把对真正爱情的追求，看成是自我价值得以实现的途径。

二

劳伦斯一生出版了 11 部诗集，近千首诗作，从而奠定了 20 世纪英国诗歌史上杰出诗人的地位。劳伦斯的诗歌是他一生中文学创作的重要组成部分，也是他一生中的欢乐与痛苦以及思想感受的重要记录。

劳伦斯的早期诗歌，具有浓厚的自传色彩，如他自己所说，这些诗篇凑在一起，构成了一部充满激情的内心生活传记。而且，他的早期诗歌具有一种内在的诚实和明快的气质，他诗中表现了画家的眼力，也表明了诗人的眼力，使诗的形象清新自然，生动逼真，具有动人美感的一面。同时，联想大胆而新鲜，比喻深刻而真切，不仅有着画家的视觉感受，还有着敏锐的触觉感受，用具有触觉的语汇来塑造抒情诗形象，触击和打动读者的心灵。

　　他在早期诗中还擅长运用象征和比喻等手法，来表现自己的观点。他常将素材重点加以暗示，并非直言。如在《农场之恋》中，他并没有告诉我们性爱与死亡在本质上是相互接近的，但他通过一系列的意象，较为笨拙的韵律和显得粗糙的情节剧的独白等手法，来使我们感觉到这种相似性。再如，在《瞧！我们走过来了！》中，劳伦斯早期生活的欢乐与痛苦也不是直接倾诉，而多半是通过诗人和弗莉达的感受来反射的。他使用的比喻颇具匠心，如在上述《农场之恋》中，他以傍晚的红霞来比喻爱情的伤痕，把张开的手臂比作举起的利剑，把双眼比作两块黑铁，把情欲比作甜蜜的火浪等等，这些比喻都恰到好处地服务了诗的主题，深化了诗的形象。

　　如果说他早期诗歌主要是自传性的记述，那么，他到了创作中期，已摆脱了这种自传的束缚，而在非人类的自然界开拓了新的诗歌的天地。他在动植物世界，以现代风格表现了现代人的感受。他1923年出版的《鸟·兽·花》，是对诗歌艺术的独特贡献，更是洋溢着生态意识的杰出的著作。《鸟·兽·花》这部诗集描述和反映各种各样的水果、树木、花朵、野兽、家禽、鸟雀等非人类的动植物的生活。这些动植物是隐喻和象征，劳伦斯通过它们来表达自己的心思、观念、情感。作为叙述者和评论者，劳伦斯经常不断地在诗中出现，因此，读着这些诗，有一种类似谈心时的愉悦；这些诗生气勃勃，清晰敏锐，措辞巧妙，富有个性。尽管这些动植物是作为隐喻和象征来使用的，但作者对它们作了生动逼真的细节描写，也作了富有力度的深层次的挖掘，使人们感到，植物有情，动物有智。

　　劳伦斯晚期的作品具有强烈的死亡意识，尤其是他晚期著名诗集《最后的诗》的中心主题。该诗集是以《凤凰》一诗结尾的，这种自行焚死，然后从灰烬中复生的凤凰意象可以说是该诗集中具有代表性的意象，也是诗人渴望身后生命的理想化身。

三

　　劳伦斯的小说与诗歌中所表达的思想和情感，是互为补充的。如《儿子与情人》所表达的情感，与劳伦斯的诗作《钢琴》十分相似。他的小说不在于讲述情节生动的故事，而是在于展现人物的心路历程。

　　同样，在长篇小说《虹》中，虹是现实与理想的结合，在劳伦斯的同名《虹》的诗歌中，虹是有两只脚的，这两只脚便是现实的根基所在。在表达性的能量方面，他的小说与诗歌更有许多相似之处，如他的诗歌《乌龟的呼喊》就表达了与他小说相似的思想。

所以，要全面理解这位"双料冠军"的创作，小说和诗歌都是缺一不可的。诗歌更集中凝练地传达他在小说中所详尽表述的思想。

英国作家劳伦斯不仅是一位出色的小说家，也是一位著名的诗人，更是一位颇受关注的画家。所以，在理解和鉴赏他的文学作品时，常常能够看到画家的影子。正是因为他是一名画家，所以，他的小说和诗歌等作品中有着强烈的触觉意识。这一触觉意识使得他的文学文本形象显得可触可摸，生动逼真。而且，更为主要的是，在劳伦斯看来，文字与图像之间的关系就如同人类文明与自然的关系一样，所以，他在自己的文学创作中追求图像效果，以图像在人与自然之间发挥一种桥梁一般的沟通作用，使得工业革命引发的人与自然出现疏远的境况得以根本改变和纠正，建立人与自然相和谐的理想关系。这也许也是他在自己的文学生涯中，将小说家兼诗人与画家的角色融为一体的一个重要原因。

尽管劳伦斯相信死亡是生命的组成部分，然而，死神是无情的，它于 1930 年夺去了劳伦斯的生命，而且也不可能让他像凤凰那样，五百年后再从灰烬中重新诞生。可是，值得九泉之下的劳伦斯庆幸的是，从某种意义上说，他以自己的艺术作品为自己制作了一条"灵船"，成为一名浴火重生的作家，就像普希金用诗歌为自己建造了一座非人工的纪念碑，他的通向黑暗的湮灭之乡的灵魂又在他的作品中萌发出来，绽放并且永存在他不朽的艺术作品之中。

吴笛

文学博士，浙江大学世界文学与比较文学研究所所长、教授、博士生导师，浙江越秀外国语学院特聘教授，兼任国家社会科学基金学科评审组专家、浙江省比较文学与外国文学学会会长，系中国作家协会会员，曾任美国斯坦福大学富布赖特研究学者。主要从事英美诗歌研究、俄罗斯诗歌研究、文学翻译研究。

D.H. LAWRENCE: A WRITER REBORN FROM THE ASHES

Wu Di

Like Thomas Hardy, D.H. Lawrence not only made a name for himself as a novelist but also established himself as one of the major poets of the 20th century. Unlike Hardy, who was so disgusted and devastated by the negative reception of *Jude the Obscure* that he stopped writing fiction and turned to poetry, publishing his first collection in his late fifties, Lawrence wrote novels alongside poetry and published his first collection in his early twenties. Lawrence was born forty-five years later than Hardy (1885), and died two years (1930) after Hardy passed on.

1

D.H. Lawrence is one of the most beloved foreign writers by Chinese readers, claiming top spots in both fiction and poetry. His novels seek to explore the blood-consciousness and blood awareness in the depth of human psyche. In novels such as *Sons and Lovers*, *The Rainbow*, *Women in Love* and *Lady Chatterley's Lover*, Lawrence displays extensive realism as well as Modernist techniques of representation.

In some of his novels, D.H. Lawrence praised the ideal relationship between man and woman, paying special attention to the spiritual and psychological development and changes of the characters. In *Sons and Lovers*, Gertrude Morel, a mental and spiritual mismatch for her miner husband, suffered a great deal from the latter's physical abuses, resulting in her concentrating all her love and attention on her sons. When Mrs Morel died, her son Paul felt that his whole life had gone with her departure, and was only able to rid himself of such conflicting feelings after a hard struggle. Evidently, what the novel discussed is not only spiritual harmony, but also the psychological 'Oedipus complex'.

Similarly, *The Rainbow* is a fictional interpretation of a family history spanning three generations. For Ursula, the heroine of the novel, it was the mind and soul that was of utmost importance. It was because of the mutual fascination of the mind that she finally abandoned the love in which mind and body are separated. What she sought was the harmonious ideal love that unites the mind and body. At the end of the novel, she finds her 'Rainbow' towering over the Earth and envisions it as the promise of a new life, a symbol of hope and rejuvenation for her future. In face of the dehumanizing power of industrialization, the reconstruction of a harmonious relationship between man and nature, especially one represented by sexual compatibility, became D.H. Lawrence's lifelong pursuit, and the rainbow imagery at the end of the novel was the symbol of this ideal relationship.

Likewise, *Women in Love*, the sequel to *The Rainbow*, depicts the loves and lives of the Brangwen sisters, Gudrun and Ursula in which they continued to search for a meaningful life in the modern world. They sought to experience emotions of primitive desire and intense love, especially the harmonious relationship and communion between the mind and body. Additionally, D.H. Lawrence attempted to describe human love from a philosophical and aesthetic perspective.

In *Lady Chatterley's Lover*, Lawrence appeared to try to rebuild the romantic myth by depicting the harmonious reunion of the mind and body rising from modern civilization. Connie, the heroine of the story, faced separation shortly after her marriage to Sir Clifford Chatterley because of World War I. Her husband went to the front line and was injured, resulting in sexual incapacitation, making him seek comfort in literary activities and philosophical questions. So, for Connie, Sir Clifford Chatterley only possessed a thinking mind, and could not be considered a human made of flesh and blood. Their relationship as husband and wife was distorted. Connie's acquaintance with Oliver Mellors, the gamekeeper, led to love despite his low social status, which she regarded as the rebirth of her femininity. Her aspiration of true love was the best way to realize self-fulfillment.

2

Throughout his life, D.H. Lawrence published 11 collections of poetry and nearly 1,000 poems, which helped establish him as one of the greatest poets in the history of English literature. Lawrence's poems are considered a significant part of his literary achievements, as well as an important record of the joys and pains in his life. They are clear presentations of his thoughts and emotions.

The early poems of Lawrence are highly autobiographical. These poems express the passionate enthusiasm of his inner life as he once mentioned. His early poems display an honest, brilliant quality, and are characterised by their picture-like descriptions and metaphors. It is the picturesque imagery full of the senses of touch and vision that arouse deep feelings in the reader.

D.H. Lawrence was skilled at using symbols and metaphors to convey his ideas, which were often not straightforwardly expressed, but rather by some kind of hint. For instance, in the poem 'Love on the Farm', he overtly states that love and death are very close in nature, but channels the similarities of love and death through imagery, rhymes and the form of dramatic monologue. Also, in the collection of poems *Look*! *We Have Come Through*, most of the joys and pains of his early life are confided through the reflection of feelings from his wife Frieda and himself. The metaphor he used is also notable. In the poem 'Love on the Farm', he compared scars of love to dusk, widespread arms to uplifted swords, a pair of eyes to two pieces of iron, sexual lust to waves of sweet fire, which highlights its theme and heightens its sensation.

In contrast to his early autobiographical poetry, in the second decade of the 20th century, D.H. Lawrence liberated himself from the bond of autobiography and developed a focus on nature. He expressed his modern ideas in the world of animals and plants. In 1923, he published a volume of poems entitled as *Birds, Beasts and Flowers*, which was a great contribution to the modern world, glittering with ecological consciousness. This volume of poems described all kinds of fruits, trees, flowers, animals, and domestic fowl. These images were often used as symbols or metaphors, through which Lawrence expressed his own ideas, points of view and emotions. As a critic and narrator, Lawrence often appeared in the poems, which makes reading them more like conversing with the author. Despite the fact that animals and plants are employed as metaphors and symbols, the poet illustrates them in great detail and depth so the reader gets the impression that plants have feelings and animals have thoughts.

The later poems of D.H. Lawrence are characterized by their deep sense of death, and this is the central theme of his famous collection *Last Poems*. This collection concludes with the poem 'Phoenix'. The image of the phoenix, burning to death and then rising from the ashes, is the representative imagery of his last volume of poems, and also the embodiment of his desire for the immortal life after death.

3

The thoughts and emotions depicted in the novels and poems of D.H. Lawrence complement one another. For example, the emotion expressed in *Sons and Lovers*, resembles that in the poem 'Piano'. His novels do not focus on telling dramatic stories, but at exhibiting the psychological journey of the characters.

In a similar sense, in his novel *The Rainbow*, the image of rainbow is the combination of reality and ideal, while in his poem entitled 'Rainbow', this image of the rainbow has its own two feet, and it is these two feet that form the root of reality. His fiction and poetry have much more in common in regard to sexual energy. In the poem 'The Tortoise Shout', for example, he expresses similar thoughts as those in his novels.

So, in order to comprehensively understand the creations of this double champion, neither novels nor poems can be ignored. His poetry, however, is a more condensed way of expressing what he details in his novels.

Besides being a famous novelist and poet, D.H. Lawrence is also known as a notable painter. So, in order to better understand and appreciate his literary works, it is necessary to know that in his literary works there are traces of his artistic qualities. Not surprisingly, there is a strong sense of touch in his literary works, making the context more real. More importantly, for Lawrence thought that the relationship between image and text were similar to that of man and nature. He sought picturesque effects in his literary creations, using the picture as a bridge between man and nature in order to correct the estranged relations, caused by the industrial revolution. His aim was to rebuild the harmonious and ideal relationship between man and nature. It is perhaps one of the reasons why he blended his identity as novelist and poet with that of his painter throughout his literary career.

D.H. Lawrence believed that the death was a part of life, but, as we know, death is merciless, and in 1930, Lawrence died. Perhaps it is impossible for him to be reborn from the ashes like the phoenix 500 years later. However, it is fortunate that in some sense, he made a 'ghost ship' with his artistic works, and in them built himself an non-artificial monument, just like Alexander Pushkin, into which his soul has arisen once again and blossomed, making him immortal through his literary works.

Wu Di

Professor, Ph.D., supervisor and dean of the Institute of World Literature and Comparative Literature, Zhejiang University. He is the commissioner of the National Funds for Social Science, member of Chinese Writer's Union, and the president of Zhejiang Provincial Association for Comparative Literature and Foreign Literature. He received his Ph.D. from Zhejiang University. He was a Fulbright research scholar at Stanford University. His research interests are English poetry, Russian poetry, and literary translation studies.

SEUM 9543   24 RUSSELL SQUA

BAF, WESTCENT, LONDON   LON

13 February 1940.

y Tandy ma'am,

     Tomorrow being the day of St.Valentine, Pries
ke the liberty of conveying my affectionate Resp
s of the family; and at the same time pass a civ
chard and to Knobs.   Wishing you many happy ret

pipes have just frozen for the third time: so I
he more benign climate of Dorset you have not su
me way; though I fear that the severity of the w
ht you hardships as well.   As I have been a vic
trouble, from which I have now recovered I beli
king Pills for Low Blood Pressure, I also hope
been visited by any epidemics or ailments.   I
ticular news, having been leading a quiet life,
y Frail health.   It is on my mind to pass by th
ottenham Court Road, where I dare say I shall fir
and wool is unobtainable; but I do not doubt tha
your hands full otherwise, and have been quite w
ne this extra chore which I imposed upon you wit
sking leave.   The Glamour Cat, I am sorry to sa
ut a suitable subject for edifying my juvenile a
she came down in the world pretty far.   The sto
and also a bit sordid.   For

he haunted many a low resort
n the dingy Road of Tottenham Court.
he flitted about the no man's land
rom the Rising Sun to the Friend at Hand.
nd the postman sighed, as he shook his head:
You'd ha' thought that cat had ought to be dead
nd who ever suppose that that
as Grizzabella, the Glamour Cat?"

V

托马斯·斯特恩斯·艾略特

THOMAS
STEARNS
ELIOT

Portrait of T.S. Eliot by John Gay, vintage print, 1948.

T.S. 艾略特肖像，约翰·盖伊摄于 1948 年，原版老照片。

托马斯·斯特恩斯·艾略特是著名的诗人、评论家、剧作家，欧美现代主义文学最重要的代表人物之一。1888年9月26日，艾略特生于美国圣路易斯的富商家庭，自幼酷爱文学，中学时代就开始创作诗歌、小说。1906年至1909年，艾略特在哈佛大学学习，开始受到象征主义文学影响。1910年至1911年，他转赴巴黎索邦大学，接触到各类欧洲前卫文化思潮。1911年至1914年又到哈佛大学攻读哲学，曾从印度学家兰曼学习梵文，师从古印度哲学研究专家吴梓学习印度哲学，师从日本学者姊崎正治学习佛学。第一次世界大战前夕，艾略特抵达伦敦。1915年，在著名诗人埃兹拉·庞德（1885～1972）的鼓励、帮助下，艾略特陆续发表了《J.阿尔弗雷德·普鲁弗洛克的情歌》等诗作，在欧美文坛初露锋芒。1919年，艾略特开始构思长诗《荒原》，1922年正式发表，轰动西方文坛，奠定了他欧美现代派诗歌开创者的崇高地位。1927年，艾略特正式皈依英国国教（圣公会）并加入英国籍。之后，他继续致力于诗歌创作，代表作有《圣灰星期三》(1930)、《擅长装扮的老猫经》(1939)、《四个四重奏》(1936～1942)等。此外他还写有多部剧本，对英国诗剧复兴运动贡献良多，如《岩石》(1934)、《大教堂谋杀案》(1935)、《家庭聚会》(1939)等。艾略特同时还是一位出色的文学评论家，其《传统与个人才能》等代表论文对英美"新批评"影响深远。1948年，艾略特获得诺贝尔文学奖。1965年1月4日，艾略特在伦敦逝世，遵照遗嘱，骨灰安葬于其祖居地英国萨默塞特郡东库克村的圣米迦勒教堂。

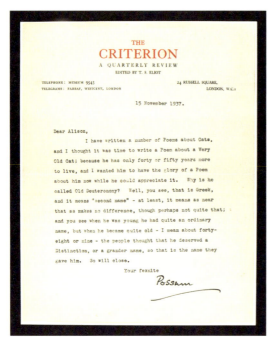

Letters and illustrations by T.S. Eliot

© Faber & Faber Ltd. and the Estate of T.S. Eliot

Letter from T.S. Eliot to Alison Tandy, dated 15 November 1937, British Library Add MS 71002 f 88r, part of 'Letters from T.S. Eliot to members of the Tandy family including drafts of poems for *Old Possum's Book of Practical Cats* 1936−40', British Library Add MS 71002, Add MS 71003.

T.S. 艾略特致艾利森·坦迪的亲笔信，信的日期为 1937 年 11 月 15 日。大英图书馆藏：Add MS 71002 f 88r.

这封信收录在"T.S. 艾略特与坦迪家族成员的书信，包括《擅长装扮的老猫经》中的诗作草稿，1936 ～ 1940 年"中。大英图书馆藏：Add MS 71002，Add MS 71003.

Envelope from T.S. Eliot to Alison Tandy, British Library Add MS 71002, f 53r.

T.S. 艾略特致艾利森·坦迪的信所用信封。大英图书馆藏：Add MS 71002，f 53r.

Letters and illustrations by T.S. Eliot

© Faber & Faber Ltd. and the Estate of T.S. Eliot

Fig.1

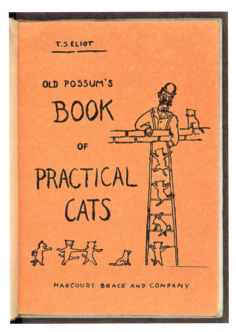

Old Possum's Book of Practical Cats by T.S. Eliot, (New York: Harcourt, Brace & Co., 1939), first American edition, British Library X.989/17707.

T.S. 艾略特著《擅长装扮的老猫经》的英文原版（纽约：哈考特与布雷斯出版公司，1939年），美国发行的第一版。大英图书馆藏：X.989/17707.

© Houghton Mifflin Harcourt and the Estate of T.S. Eliot

Thomas Stearns Eliot (1888–1965) was friends with Geoffrey Tandy, the marine biologist and broadcaster. Eliot corresponded with the Tandy family, including Polly, Geoffrey's wife, and daughters Alison and Anthea, to whom Eliot was godfather. After Anthea passed away the letters and poems remained in an attic until her husband, Edward Kinder discovered them in 1991. Many of the letters contain poetry by Eliot, including drafts of poems which would be published in *Old Possum's Book of Practical Cats* in 1939. **[Fig. 1]**

托马斯·斯特恩斯·艾略特和杰弗里·坦迪是好朋友，坦迪是一名海洋生物学家，也是节目主持人。艾略特长期与坦迪一家通信，包括杰弗里的妻子波利和女儿艾丽森与安西娅——艾略特是这两位姑娘的教父。安西娅去世后，这些信件和诗作手稿都被存放在阁楼里，她的丈夫爱德华·肯德直到1991年才发现它们。许多信件中有艾略特的诗作，包括收录在1939年出版的诗集《擅长装扮的老猫经》中的诗稿。（图1）

Writing on 15 November 1937, Eliot told Alison Tandy that 'I have written a number of Poems about Cats, and I thought it was time to write a Poem about a Very Old Cat; because he has only forty or fifty years more to live, and I wanted him to have the glory of a Poem about him now while he could appreciate it'. Eliot included a version of the poem 'Old Deuteronomy' which was published in *Old Possum's Book of Practical Cats* with some minor changes. The last two lines of the second verse were published as 'My sight's unreliable, but I can guess That the cause of the trouble is Old Deuteronomy!' while Eliot's letter to Tandy reads 'My sight's not reliable, but I can guess That the interruption is Old Deuteronomy!'. **[Fig. 2]** Eliot clearly found cats amusing and he provided advice to Polly Tandy about a cat called Misterperkins on 9 December 1936, writing 'When a Cat adopts you ... there is nothing to be done about it ... you must for the present provide liver and rabbit, and a comfortable seat by the fire'. **[Fig. 3]**

1937 年 11 月 15 日，艾略特在信中对艾丽森说道："我写过很多关于猫的诗，如今我想写篇关于很老很老的猫的诗。这只猫顶多再活个四五十年了，我想趁他还能品味诗歌的时候在诗中给予他赞颂。"艾略特在《擅长装扮的老猫经》中加入了略微改动过的《老戒律伯》一诗，诗的第二篇最后两行原本印刷的是"我的眼神不济事儿了，可我能猜到惹事的主儿肯定是老戒律伯！"而艾略特在信中却写的是"我的视力靠不住了，但我还是能猜想这其中的障碍就是老戒律伯！"（图 2）

艾略特显然是很喜欢猫，他在 1936 年 12 月 9 日寄给波利·坦迪的一封信里，针对一只名叫"米斯特珀金"的猫给出了建议。他写道："当一只猫认定了你……就没有办法了……你当务之急必须要准备好肝脏和兔肉，还有一个炉火边的舒服座位。"（图 3）

Fig.2

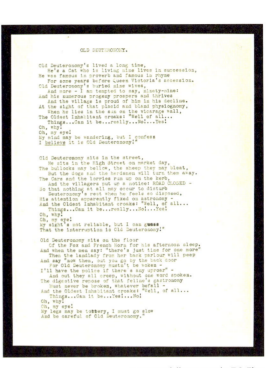

Draft of poem 'Old Deuteronomy' by T.S. Eliot in a letter from Eliot to Alison Tandy, dated 15 November 1937, British Library Add MS 71002, f 89r.

《老戒律伯》一诗的草稿，T.S. 艾略特作，夹在艾略特写给艾利森·坦迪的信中，信的日期为 1938 年 11 月 15 日。大英图书馆藏：Add MS 71002，f 89r.

Letters and illustrations by T.S. Eliot

© Faber & Faber Ltd. and the Estate of T.S. Eliot

Fig.3

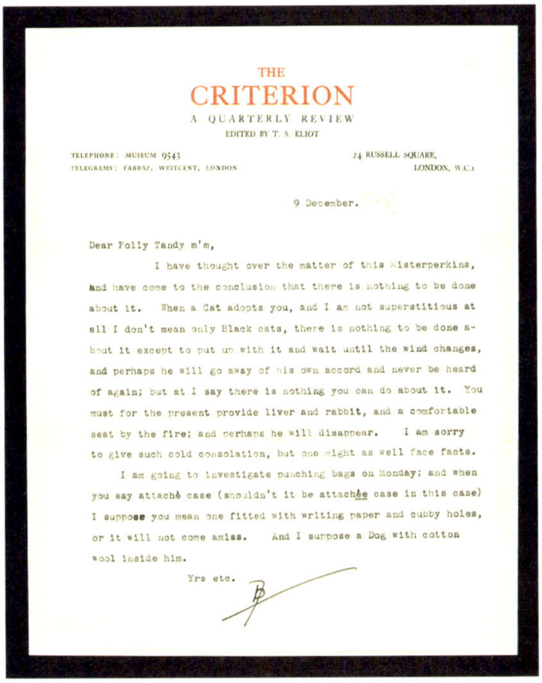

Letter from T.S. Eliot to Polly Tandy, dated 9 December [1936], British Library Add MS 71002, f 53r.

T.S. 艾略特致波利·坦迪的信，信的日期为 [1936 年] 12 月 9 日。大英图书馆藏：Add MS 71002，f 53r.

Letters and illustrations by T.S. Eliot

© Faber & Faber Ltd. and the Estate of T.S. Eliot

These letters contain vestiges of characters and poems which Eliot did not always use. One letter, f 45, written on the day before Valentine's Day in 1940, is annotated with hearts and a cartoon figure with a cupid's arrow through its heart. Eliot shares part of a poem about Grizabella, the Glamour Cat, stating 'The Glamour Cat, I am sorry to say, is not turning out a suitable subject for edifying my juvenile audience; in fact, she came down in the world pretty far. The story is very sad, and also a bit sordid. For:

She haunted many a low resort
In the dingy road of Tottenham Court.
She flitted about the no man's land
From the Rising Sun to the Friend at Hand.
And the postman sighed, as he shook his head:
"You'd ha' thought that cat had ought to be dead"

And who ever suppose that that
Was Grizabella, the Glamour Cat?'

这些信件中包含的一些形象和诗歌的只言片语都是艾略特所不常使用的。例如第45页这封信，它作于1940年情人节前一天，信纸上竟画有几颗桃心，还有个被丘比特之箭刺穿胸膛的漫画小人。艾略特在信中分享了一部分关于"过气的魅力猫"格里泽贝拉的故事："我很遗憾地告诉你们，我写的那只过气的魅力猫，对于我的青年读者来说毫无教育意义；而且事实上，它变得十分潦倒、落魄。这是个悲伤的故事，甚至有些丑恶。因为：

她出没在托敦汉短巷周围的
许多肮脏地段
她流浪在无人地区
从'如日中天'到'四处乞讨'
而邮差抓抓头叹口气
'你一定想过这只猫早该死去'
而有谁会想到
那就是当年妖艳的格里泽贝拉？ [1]"

Fig.4

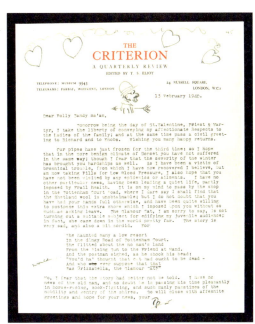

Letter from T.S. Eliot to Polly Tandy, dated 13 February 1940, British Library Add MS 71003, f 45r.

T.S. 艾略特致波利·坦迪的信，信的日期为 1940 年 2 月 13 日。大英图书馆藏：Add MS 71003，f 45r.

Letters and illustrations by T.S. Eliot

© Faber & Faber Ltd. and the Estate of T.S. Eliot

He goes on to write 'No, I fear that the story had better not be told'. [Fig. 4]

And true to his word, Eliot did not feature Grizabella in *Old Possum's Book of Practical Cats* as it was considered too sad for children. However, Eliot's wife, Valerie, shared a fragment of the poem with the musician Andrew Lloyd Webber, and the character of Grizabella was given a prominent role in his 1981 musical *Cats*.

他接着又写道："不，我觉得还是不要讲这个故事了。"（图 4）

艾略特没有食言，他后来果真没有把格里泽贝拉写进《擅长装扮的老猫经》里，因为对于孩子们来说这个故事太过悲伤了。不过，艾略特的妻子瓦莱丽曾向音乐剧作家安德鲁·劳埃德·韦伯出示过这首诗的片断，于是后来在韦伯 1981 年创作的音乐剧《猫》中，格里泽贝拉成了一个重要的角色。

1　艾略特《猫》，费元洪译，上海译文出版社，2012 年，第 20 页。

艾略特作品在中国
Thomas Stearns Eliot's works in China

  由于艾略特的作品较为深奥晦涩，再加上他身兼诗人、评论家的双重身份，创作与理论相辅相成，艾略特作品在中国的译介、评论从一开始就带有鲜明的理论性、学术性倾向。20世纪三四十年代，在北大、清华以及后来的西南联大校园中，艾略特的诗作、文论风行一时，深刻影响了一批从事诗歌创作与研究的青年学子，如卞之琳、赵萝蕤、王佐良、查良铮（穆旦）、袁可嘉等，他们大多在当时及日后为艾略特作品的译介与研究做出了巨大的贡献。到20世纪中叶，作为西方现代主义文学代表人物的艾略特在中国内地遭到简单否定，但译介仍不绝如缕；而在同时期的港台地区，对艾略特的译介、研究仍一直在进行，对这一时期中文现代诗的发展产生了不可忽略的影响。20世纪80年代初以来，艾略特作品的译介、研究在中国内地逐步复兴，出现了前所未有的繁荣局面。

作品译介
Translations

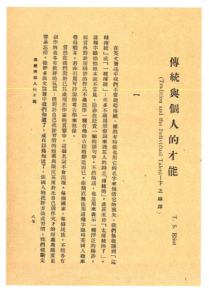

《传统与个人的才能》，卞之琳译，《学文》第一卷第一期，1934 年。
'Tradition and the Individual Talent', trans. by Bian Zhilin,
Xue Wen, Vol. 1, No. 1, 1934.

　　从 20 世纪 30 年代开始，在叶公超等学者的大力推动和鼓励下，大批中国文人、学者开始投身艾略特作品的翻译工作。卞之琳曾如此回忆："叶公超是第一个引起我对二三十年代艾略特、晚期叶芝、左倾的奥顿等英美现代派诗风兴趣的人。" 1934 年，卞之琳应叶公超之请，翻译了艾略特的文论名篇《传统与个人的才能》，发表于《学文》月刊。之后，曹葆华、李赋宁等学人也重译过此文，对中国文坛影响深远。

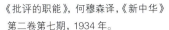

《批评的职能》，何穆森译，《新中华》
第二卷第七期，1934 年。
'The Function of Criticism', trans.
by He Musen, *Xin Zhong Hua* (*New
China*), Vol. 2, No. 7, 1934.

《批评的机构》，京夏译，《文艺》第四
卷第四期，1936 年。
'The Function of Criticism', trans.
by Jing Xia, *Wen Yi*, Vol. 4, No. 4,
1936.

　　1934 年，何穆森翻译了艾略特的另一篇著名文论《批评的职能》，发表于《新中华》杂志。1936 年，成都出版的《文艺》杂志又刊登了署名"京夏"的译文，题为《批评的机构》，末附后记，简略介绍了艾略特的生平、作品与文艺见解。

《"诗的用处与批评的用处"序说》，周煦良译，《现代诗风》1935 年第 1 期。

Introduction to *The Use of Poetry and the Use of Criticism*, trans. by Zhou Xuliang, *Xian Dai Shi Feng* (*Modern Poetical Trends*), No. 1, 1935.

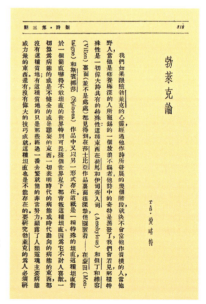

《诗与宣传》，周煦良译，《新诗》1936 年第 1 期。

'Poetry and Propaganda', trans. by Zhou Xuliang, *New Poetry*, No. 1, 1936.

《勃莱克论》，周煦良译，《新诗》1936 年第三期。

'William Blake', trans. by Zhou Xuliang, *New Poetry*, No. 3, 1936.

1935 年至 1936 年，周煦良（1905～1984）先后翻译了爱略特（艾略特）的三篇文论：《"诗的用处与批评的用处"序说》《诗与宣传》《勃莱克论》，发表于《现代诗风》《新诗》杂志。此外同一时期发表的艾略特文论译文还有白云译《诗与宣传》，赵增厚、光祖选译《诗的功用与批评的功用》等。

《现代诗论》，曹葆华译，商务印书馆，1937 年。
Essays on Modern Poetical Theories, trans. by Cao Baohua,
the Commercial Press, 1937.

　　1937 年，诗人、翻译家曹葆华将自己翻译的 14 篇西方诗学理论文章结集为《现代诗论》，由上海商务印书馆出版。书中收录了爱略式（艾略特）的《传统与个人才能》《批评底功能》《批评中的试验》等 3 篇文章。曹葆华在序言中把艾略特和梵乐希（通译瓦莱里）称为"现代英法两个最伟大的诗人，同时又都是这两国最重要的批评家"，认为他们的诗论"与他们的创作是分不开的"，还在文后案语中简要概括、评述了艾略特的观点。

黄宗英编《赵萝蕤汉译〈荒原〉手稿》，高等教育出版社，2013 年。

A Facsimile and Transcript of the Original Draft of Zhao Luorui's Translation of T.S. Eliot's the Waste Land into Chinese in 1936, edited & introduced by Huang Zongying, Higher Education Press, 2013.

年 6 月我收到了 10 本简装本和若干豪华本。这本书计印行了简装 300 本，豪华 50 本。豪华本定价 8 角。1937 年 7 月卢沟桥事变，我与家人便离开了北京。刚收到的书除自留几本外，一般脑儿交到东安市场的中原书店里。

大概是在昆明的时候，读到了 1939 年上海《西洋文学》邢光祖先生的文章，详细评介了艾略特的这首杰作，也评述了我的译文，我有幸至今还保存着这唯一的一篇学术性很强的评论文章。在昆明的六七年中，我还曾受重庆《时事新报》"学灯"版宗白华先生之托，写了一篇《艾略特与荒原》的文章。

1944 年秋，蒙家与我到美国芝加哥大学落脚。1946 年 7 月蒙家在哈佛大学会见了回美国探亲的艾略特，并打电报给我立刻起程东行到哈佛与艾略特见面。7 月 9 日晚上艾略特请我在哈佛俱乐部晚餐，晚餐后他为我朗读了《四个四重奏》中的片断，并嘱我下一个任务就是翻译这首和《荒原》的风格很不相同的长诗。他还为我带去的两本书：《1909—1935 年诗歌集》和《四个四重奏》签上他的名字。在前者的扉页上他写了"为赵萝蕤签名，感谢她翻译了荒原"。他还给了我两张照片并在上面签上了名字。这两张照片后来在多次的抄家中丢失了。蒙家告诉他我也写了许多诗，他听了十分高兴，建议我把它们译成英文，先在英国出版。当时我把我写的诗抄在一个本上，但后来它遇到了照片同样的命运，没有留下片言只字。

在我们交谈之际，我十分留意察看这位与同十分渊博诗艺又确实精湛的奇人，他高高瘦瘦的个子，腰背微驼，声音不是清亮而是相当低沉，神色不是安详而似乎稍稍有些紧张，好像前面还有什么不能预测的东西。那年他 58 岁。

1948 年冬我登上了回国的航程，船上的广播还在报告北京西郊的燕京与清华已经解放。我于 12 月 31 日到达上海，两个星期后乘一架运粮食的飞机降落在天坛的一块空地上。此后度过了忙

赵萝蕤回忆艾略特，见《我的读书生涯》，北京大学出版社，1996 年。

'Zhao Luorui's recollection of her meeting with T.S. Eliot in 1946,' in *My Reading Life*, Peking University Press, 1996.

　　《荒原》1922 年发表之后，为艾略特带来了巨大声望，至今仍被视为 20 世纪最重要、最有影响力的诗作。全诗内容极为复杂艰深，广泛涉及了欧洲各国以至印度的神话、宗教、哲学、文学、历史等各方面的形象、典故，诗中除了英文之外，还出现了德文、法文、意大利文、拉丁文、希腊文以至梵文等多种文字，翻译难度可想而知。1935 年，正在清华大学外国文学研究所攻读硕士学位的赵萝蕤（1912～1998）试译了《荒原》的第一节。1936 年，赵萝蕤应戴望舒约请，翻译了《荒原》全篇和诗人原注，并在美籍教授温德指导下作了详细译注，赵萝蕤的恩师叶公超亲自为该译本作序，于 1937 年夏出版。这是该篇重要诗作的第一个中文全译本，它的问世成为当时中国文坛的一桩盛事。1946 年 7 月，赵萝蕤在美国哈佛大学俱乐部曾与艾略特共进晚餐。艾略特将有自己签名的诗集赠送给她，在扉页上写了"为赵萝蕤签署"，感谢她翻译《荒原》。席间，艾略特还为她朗诵了自己的《四个四重奏》片断，希望她能将这一部作品也译成中文。虽然这一意愿后来由于种种原因未能实现，却仍可谓 20 世纪中外文学交流史上的一段佳话。

《古波斯僧的旅行》，邹绿芷译，《诗垦地丛刊》第四期，1942 年。
'Journey of the Magi' trans. by Zou Lüzhi, *Shi Ken Di Cong Kan* (*The Upturned Soil of Poetry*), No. 4, 1942.

《亚尔佛列德·普鲁佛洛克底恋歌》，黎敏子译，《诗创作》第十六期，1942 年。
'The Love Song of J. Alfred Prufrock', trans. by Li Minzi, *Shi Chuang Zuo* (*Poetical Composition*), No. 16, 1942.

　　即使是在抗战与内战的烽火中，中国文学界对艾略特的兴趣依旧不减。如 1937 年 8 月南京《文艺月刊》登载了朱文振译《某女史小像》；1942 年，在大后方四川出版的《诗垦地丛刊》第四期所刊邹绿芷译《现代英国诗抄》中包括了《古波斯僧的旅行》；同年桂林出版的《诗创作》杂志发表了黎敏子译《亚尔佛列德·普鲁佛洛克底恋歌》，"译后记"认为此诗深刻表现了"代表整个没落的贵族的阶级"的主人公在新时代的"彷徨和焦急"。

《东柯刻》，李嘉译，《诗音丛刊》第一期，1947 年。
'East Coker', trans. by Li Jia, *Shi Yin Cong Kan*
(*Poetical Voice Magazine*), No. 1, 1947.

　　第二次世界大战前不久至战争期间，艾略特陆续创作发表了他最为成熟的代表作《四个四重奏》(1936 ～ 1942) [1]。仅仅数年之后，这部长诗的前两部分就已经有了中译文。1946 年 2 月，李嘉在印度新德里翻译了其中的第二篇《东柯刻》，发表于 1947 年 2 月在上海出版的《诗音丛刊》。稍后不久，著名的"九叶派"诗人唐湜翻译了全诗首篇《燃烧了的诺顿》，发表于《诗创造》杂志第十期。同期还刊载了英国著名诗人、评论家史彭德的评论文章《T.S. 艾略忒的"四个四重奏"》(岑鄂之译)、《近年英国诗之一瞥》(陈敬容译)。

1　共包含四部分：《焚毁的诺顿》(Burnt Norton，1936)；《东库克》(East Coker，1940)；《干赛尔维其斯》(The Dry Salvages，1941)；《小吉丁》(Little Gidding，1942)，1943 年出版单行本。

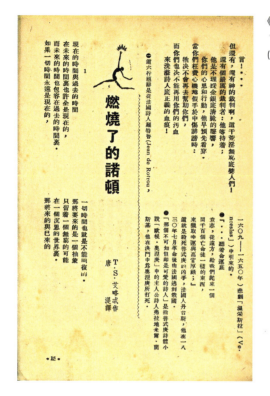

《燃烧了的诺顿》，唐湜译，《诗创造》第十期，1948 年。
'Burnt Norton', trans. by Tang Shi, *Shi Chuang Zao*
(*Poetical Creation*), No. 10, 1948.

史彭德《T.S. 艾略忒的 "四个四重奏"》，岑鄂之译，《诗
创造》第十期，1948 年。
'On T.S. Eliot's "The Four Quartets"' by Stephen
Spender, trans. by Cen E'zhi, *Shi Chuang Zao*
(*Poetical Creation*), No. 10, 1948.

《爱伦·坡在文学上的地位》，许天虹译，《改进》第十一卷第四期，1945 年。
'A Dream within a Dream'（T.S. Eliot on Edgar Allan Poe）, trans. by Xu Tianhong, *Gai Jin*（*Advancement*）, Vol. 11, No. 4, 1945.

《路狄雅德·吉卜林》，荃里译，《文艺先锋》第十二卷第六期，1948 年。
'Rudyard Kipling', trans. by Quan Li, *Vanguards of Literature and Art*, Vol. 12, No. 6, 1948.

　　同一时期发表的艾略特作品译文还有许天虹译《爱伦·坡在文学上的地位》、荃里译《路狄雅德·吉卜林》等。

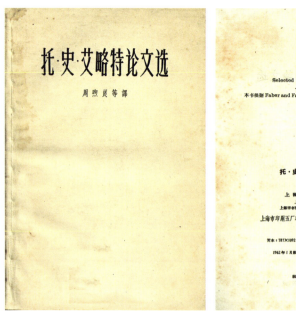

《托·史·艾略特论文选》(内部发行),周煦良等译,上海文艺出版社,1962 年。
Selected Essays of T.S. Eliot, trans. by Zhou Xuliang etc., Shanghai Literature and Arts Press, 1962.

20 世纪五六十年代,西方现代主义文艺在中国内地几乎遭到全面否定。艾略特既是欧美现代主义文学的代表人物,又在政治、社会等方面持基督教保守主义立场,自称"文学上是古典主义者,政治上是君主派,宗教上是圣公会公教徒"[1],因而更是被"打入另册"。然而即使在这段特殊的历史时期,对艾略特作品的译介也并未完全中断。1962 年,上海文艺出版社以"内部发行"名义出版了周煦良等翻译的《托·史·艾略特论文选》,这可能是这一时期中国内地出版的唯一——部艾略特著作译本。

1　"The general point of view﹝of the essays﹞may be described as classicist in literature, royalist in politics, and anglo-catholic in religion," in preface by T.S. Eliot to *For Lancelot Andrewes*：*Essays on style and order* (1929).

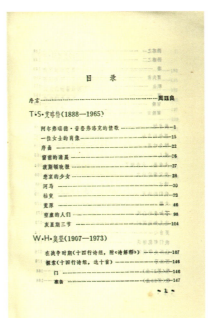

《英国现代诗选》，查良铮（穆旦）译，湖南人民出版社，1985 年。
Selected Modern English Poetry, trans. and annotated by Zha
Liangzheng（Mu Dan），Hunan People's Publishing House，1985.

　　"文革"后期，严酷的政治、文化环境开始稍有松动。1973 至 1977 年，著名诗人、翻译家查良铮（穆旦）在出版尚无指望的情况下，翻译了艾略特、奥登等英国现代诗人的作品。译稿起初仅在极少数亲友、弟子间传阅，身后由其内兄、著名翻译家周珏良编成《英国现代诗选》出版。查良铮早在 20 世纪 40 年代就深受艾略特、奥登等人影响，译本中包括了艾略特的《阿尔弗瑞德·普鲁弗洛克的情歌》《一位女士的肖像》《荒原》《空虚的人们》《灰星期三节》等重要诗作，他还根据能够得到的各种资料作了详细的译注。[1]

1　如布鲁克斯、华伦《了解诗歌》（1950 年版）、吉尔伯特·费尔普斯编《问答》（剑桥大学出版社 1969 年版）等。

改革开放之后，赵萝蕤修订了《荒原》的译文及注释，发表于《外国文艺》1980 年第 3 期。同期还刊登了曹庸翻译的《传统与个人才能》；同年出版的《外国现代派作品选》第一册收录了查良铮译《阿尔弗瑞德·普鲁弗洛克的情歌》、赵萝蕤译《荒原》，由袁可嘉撰写引言，标志着中国内地对艾略特的译介正式开始复苏。此后，中国国内兴起了新一轮艾略特译介、研究的热潮。不仅是卞之琳、赵萝蕤、袁可嘉等前辈参与其中，赵毅衡、裘小龙、汤永宽等新一代译者也作出了巨大的贡献。

赵萝蕤译《荒原》(修订译本)，《外国文艺》1980 年第 3 期。
The Waste Land, a revised translation by Zhao Luorui, in *Foreign Literature*, No. 3, 1980.

《外国现代派作品选》(第一册) 中的艾略特作品引言，上海文艺出版社，1980 年。
Selected Foreign Modernist Literary Works Vol. 1, Shanghai Literature and Arts Press, 1980.

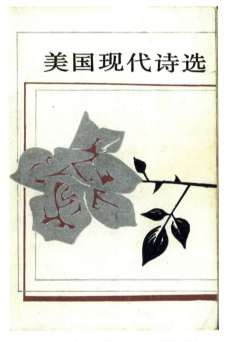

《美国现代诗选》，赵毅衡译，外国文学出版社，1985年。
Selected Modern American Poetry，trans. by Zhao Yiheng，
Foreign Literature Publishing House，1985.

《四个四重奏》，裘小龙译，漓江出版社，1985 年。
Four Quartets and Other Poems, trans. by Qiu Xiaolong, Lijiang Press, 1985.

《情歌·荒原·四重奏》，汤永宽译，上海译文出版社，1994 年。
'*Love Song*', '*Waste Land*' and '*Quartets*', trans. by Tang Yongkuan, Shanghai Translation Publishing House, 1994.

《荒原·四首四重奏》，杜若洲译，台
湾志文出版社，1985年。
'*The Waste Land*' and '*Four Quartets*', trans. by Du Ruozhou,
Zhi Wen Press（Taipei）. 1985.

在中国内地之外，台湾、香港等地区的艾略特译介和研究也从未间断，重要译本有叶维
廉译《诺贝尔文学奖全集·艾略特卷》、杜若洲译《荒原·四首四重奏》等。

《艾略特文学论文集》，李赋宁译，百花洲文艺出版社，1994 年。

Literary Essays of T.S. Eliot, trans. by Li Funing, Baihuazhou Literature and Art Publishing House, 1994.

《基督教与文化》，杨民生、陈常锦译，汪淼校，四川人民出版社，1989 年。

Christianity and Culture, trans. by Yang Minsheng, Chen Changjin, Sichuan People's Press，1989.

《艾略特文集》(五卷)，上海译文出版社，2012 年。
Collected Works of T.S. Eliot, 5 Vols. Shanghai Translation Publishing House, 2012.

　　值得一提的是，半个多世纪间，仅仅《荒原》就至少出现了五六种全译本，这在中国文坛和翻译界均不多见，可谓艾略特作品在当代中国传播的特点与亮点，从中亦可看出艾略特对于中国文坛影响之深远。而 20 世纪 80 年代至今，中国对艾略特作品的译介在广度、深度上都有了空前的进步，译介范围包含了诗作、文论以至宗教、文化方面的论著。2012 年上海译文出版社出版了五卷本《艾略特文集》，收入了艾略特的诗歌、戏剧、文论等绝大部分作品，成为艾略特译介史上的里程碑。

评论研究
Reviews

"玄"（茅盾）《几个消息》，《文学》（《文学旬刊》）第 85 期，1923 年。
T.S. Eliot's name was mentioned in 'Several Pieces of News' by 'Xuan'（Mao Dun），*Literature Periodical*，No. 85，1923.

R.D. Jameson《诗与本义：艾略特诗学方法札记》，《清华学报》第七卷第一期，1932 年。
'Poetry and Plain Sense（A Note on the Poetic Method of T.S. Eliot）' by R.D. Jameson，*The Tsing Hua Journal*，Vol. 7，No. 1，1932.

　　在艾略特的名作《荒原》问世后不久，他的名字就已传入了中国。1923年8月27日，茅盾以笔名"玄"在《时事新报》副刊《文学》上发表简讯《几个消息》，报道了几则欧美文坛动态，其中提到此年6月英国 *Adelphi* 杂志创刊，"英国现代文人如 D.H. Lawrence，Arnold Bennett，T.S. Eliot 等都是撰稿员"。根据现有资料，这是艾略特的名字第一次出现在中国文学界视野之中。1927年，朱自清翻译了清华大学教授 R.D. Jameson 的文章《纯粹的诗》(Pure Poetry)，发表于《小说月报》第18卷第20号，文章首尾两段都将艾略特与格特鲁德·斯坦因、保罗·瓦莱里等并列为"现代欧洲诸著作家"的代表。1932年，R.D. Jameson 还在《清华学报》上发表文章，论述艾略特的诗学方法。

《吴宓日记》1931 年 1 月 20 日，生活·读书·新知三联书店，1998 年。
Wu Mi on his meeting with T.S. Eliot, Jan. 20, 1931, in
The Daries of Wu Mi, SDX Joint Publishing Company, 1998.

一月二十日　星期二

　　阴。微雨。　晨，作函致贤，大意言贤与宓性情兴趣相同，极适为配偶，但既各有所恋，而宓必忠于恋爱，故决婚彦。明知彦不合宓之理想，但婚姻乃实际关系，故愿实行 Give to Caesar things that belong to Caesar；Give to God things that belong to God ④ 之办法。知我前后始末之最高心理者，唯贤而已，云云。(函系英文)。

　　11—1 至博文堂 Arthur Prosthain, Oriental Booksellers, 41 Great Russell Street, W. C.1 ⑤ 与书店主人谈甚久。其人年五十，为德国犹太人，见解颇超俗。因与约定代售《学衡》，及送书备《文副》批评介绍之办法。并以浦江清君之名写与之。

　　1—3 访 T. S. Eliot(仍见其女书记，伤其美而作工，未嫁)，邀宓步至附近之 Cosmo Hotel ⑥ 午餐，谈。Eliot 君自言与白璧德师主张相去较近，而与 G. K. Chesterton ⑦ 较远。但以公布发表之文章观之，则似若适得其反云。又以书名片，介绍宓见英、法文士多人，不赘记。

　　下午三时半，至 Westminster 国会旁听。是日为本年开会第一日。议事日程另存。初议星期三增加会议案，反对党多施攻击，杂以笑谑。继议庚款案 The China(Education) Box Indemnity Bill ②。反对党虽有驳诘，实皆中事理，反复周详，其精神至为可佩。宓直坐听至九时后，俟庚款案二读通过，乃出。遇王兆俊君及使馆之邱君，则未终席而去。另有中国男女学生二人在座。宓思彦不肯来欧，藉口为人訾笑，殊不成理由。宓至国民楼晚餐地见前。(2S.)。归寝。

　　1931 年，著名学者、诗人、"学衡派"代表人物吴宓在伦敦访问了同为白璧德弟子的艾略特，艾略特还为吴宓"书名片，介绍宓见英、法文士多人"。吴宓在日记中记录"Eliot 君自言与白璧德师主张相去较近，而与 G.K. Chesterton[1] 较远。但以公布发表之文章观之，则似若适得其反云"。回国后，吴宓在 1937 至 1938 年开设《文学与人生》课程，不止一次提及艾略特之名，并引述了《传统与个人才能》《但丁》等文论。

1　G.K. 切斯特顿（1874～1936），英国作家、批评家，著有小说《布朗神父探案集》，评论著作《狄更斯评传》《萧伯纳评传》，神学著作《回到正统》《永恒的人》及大量随笔、诗歌等。1922 年皈依天主教。

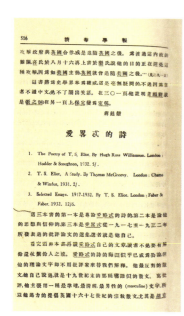

叶公超《爱略忒的诗》,《清华学报》第九卷第二期, 1934 年。

'On T.S. Eliot's Poems' by Ye Gongchao, *The Tsing Hua Jouranal*, Vol. 9, No. 2, 1934.

叶公超《再论爱略特的诗》,《北平晨报·文艺》, 1937 年 4 月 5 日。

'More Remarks on T.S. Eliot's Poems' by Ye Gongchao (an introduction to the Chinese version of 'The Waste Land' trans. by Zhao Luorui), on *Bei Ping Chen Bao* (*Beiping Morning News*), April 5, 1937.

中国第一位真正全面介绍艾略特文学成就的批评家当属叶公超。叶公超早年留学英国期间就与艾略特相熟，彼此交流甚多。他曾回忆，"我在英国时，常和他（指艾略特）见面，跟他很熟。大概第一个介绍艾氏的诗与诗论给中国的，就是我"，甚至还一度"希望自己也能写出一首像《荒原》这样的诗，可以表现出我国从诗经时代到现在的生活"[1]，徐志摩也曾半开玩笑地将叶公超称为"一个 T.S. 艾略特的信徒"[2]。1934 年，叶公超在《清华学报》上发表书评《爱略式的诗》，借评介艾略特《批评论文选集》(*Selected Essays: 1917–1932*) 和两种研究著作的机会，着重分析了艾略特的诗歌创作理念与诗学观，阐述了叶公超自己对这位大诗人的看法，认为艾略特的方法"是要造成一种扩大错综的知觉，要表现整个文明的心灵，要理解过去的存在性"。而在几年后为赵萝蕤译《荒原》所作的序文《再论爱略特的诗》中，叶公超不仅全面评价了艾略特的诗学造诣与文学贡献，还将他的诗学主张与中国诗学传统进行了比较，认为"他的影响之大竟令人感觉，也许将来他的诗本身的价值还不及他的影响的价值呢"。

1　叶公超《文学·艺术·永不退休》(原载 1979 年 3 月 15 日台北《中国时报》副刊)，见陈子善编《叶公超批评文集》第 266 页（珠海出版社，1998 年）
2　叶公超为悼念胡适所作《深夜怀友》(原载 1962 年 3 月 1 日《文星》第九卷第五期)，见《叶公超批评文集》第 245 页。

温源宁《现代英美四大诗人》,《青年界》第三卷第二期,1932 年。

'Four Great Modern Poets of Britain and United States' by Wen Yuanning, *Qing Nian Jie* (*Youth World*), Vol. 2, No. 2, 1932.

 1932 年,温源宁在《现代英美四大诗人》中,称艾略特为"了解一切"的诗人,将他对现代社会的态度概括为"没有法子可以逃避我们的时代,且让我们真能懂得它","理解的瞬间也就是解脱,自由和当我们自己命运的主人的瞬间"。1934 年 10 月,邵洵美在《现代》杂志发表《现代美国诗坛概观》一文,较为全面地介绍了艾略特及其代表作《荒原》的艺术特点,认为艾略特的诗"不被国界所限制","简直还不受时间的限制"。

赵萝蕤《艾略特与〈荒原〉》,收入《我的读书生涯》。

'T.S. Eliot and *The Waste Land*' by Zhao Luorui, in *My Reading Life*.

 这一时期,赵萝蕤除了翻译《荒原》之外,还撰写了《艾略特与〈荒原〉》一文,全面评析了艾略特诗歌的艺术特色,从语言节奏、用典、对衬反讽等方面探讨了《荒原》的艺术成就。

邢光祖《赵萝蕤译〈荒原〉书评》，《西洋文学》1940 年第 4 期。
'Book Review：Zhao Luorui's Translation of T.S. Eliot's *the Waste Land*' by Xing Guangzu, *Western Literature*, No. 4, 1940.

　　1940 年 12 月，邢光祖在上海《西洋文学》杂志发表了《荒原》赵萝蕤译本的书评，在叶公超等前辈学者的基础上，进一步分析了艾略特和苏轼、严羽等宋人之间持论的相似之处，认为艾略特的诗跟詹姆斯·乔伊斯的小说一样，"都以'委曲'作手段的"；提出翻译他的诗可以补救中国新诗创作中过分热情洋溢的倾向，"锻练我们的批判才能"；同时推崇赵萝蕤能忠实直译，"绝无一丝儿曲解原意的地方"，"译者和原作者已是化而为一"，达到了"翻译的最高标准"。

西窗 (In imitation of T. S. Eliot.)

仙鶴

（一）

这西窗
这不知趣的西窗放進
一條條直的斜的犀躺在我的床上；
闰月天時下午三點鐘的陽光
放進一圈搗亂的風片
漫住了難免處女羞的花窗簾，
阿她瘙腰溽弄脖子上，
蓋得她直瞪在牛簽寒，刮破了臉；
放進下面走道上洗被單
襴衣大小叩巾的膩子昧

（二）

廚房裏飯腥魚腥蒜苗是腐乳的沁芳南
還有弄堂裏的人聲比狗叫更顯得鬆脆。
常然不知越也不止是這西窗，
但這西窗是夠頑皮的
它何嘗不知道這是人們打中覺的好時光——
拿一件衣服，不拿這條繡外國花的毛毯
給堵死了它給悶死了它
耶穌死了我們也好睡覺！
直著身子不好彎着來，
學一只賣弄風騷的大龍蝦，
在清淺的水灘上引誘水波的蕩菑——

仙鹤（徐志摩）《西窗：In imitation of T.S. Eliot》，《新月》第一卷第四期，1928 年。
'West Window：In imitation of T.S. Eliot' by Xu Zhimo, *Xin Yue* (*Crescent Moon*), Vol. 1, No. 4, 1928.

歸

像一個天文家離開了望遠鏡，
從熱鬧中出來聞自己的足音。
莫非在自己圈子外的圈子外？
伸向黃昏去的路像一段灰心。

一月？日

卞之琳《归》，见《鱼目集》，文化生活出版社，1936 年。
'Return' by Bian Zhilin, in *Yu Mu Ji* (*Fish Eyes*), Cultural Life Press, 1936.

艾略特《阿尔弗瑞德·普鲁弗洛克的情歌》
"街连着街，好象一场讨厌的争议……"，
《外国现代派作品选》，上海文艺出版社，
1980 年。
An excerpt of 'The Love Song of J. Alfred
Prufrock', trans. by Zha Liangzheng (Mu
Dan), in *Selected Foreign Modernist
Literary Works*, Shanghai Literature and
Arts Press, 1980.

假如我认为，我是回答
一个能转回阳世间的人，
那么这火焰就不会再摇闪。
但既然，如我听到的果真，
没有人能活着离开这深渊，
我回答你就不必害怕流言。

那么我们走吧，你我两个人，
正当朝天空慢慢铺展着黄昏
好似病人麻醉在手术桌上；
我们走吧，穿过一些半冷清的街，
那儿休憩的场所正人声喋喋；
有夜夜不宁的下等歇夜旅店
和满地蚌壳的铺锯末的饭馆，
街连着街，好象一场讨厌的争议
带有阴险的意图
要把你引向一个重大的问题……
唉，不要问，"那是什么？"
让我们快点走去作客。

　　20 世纪 20 年代至 40 年代，像徐志摩、邵洵美、何其芳、孙大雨、王辛笛、戴望舒、穆旦等一大批中国诗人都或多或少受过艾略特的影响。例如徐志摩在《新月》第一卷第四期发表了一首题为《西窗》的诗，该作的副标题便是："仿 T.S. 艾略特"；又如卞之琳《归》中的名句"伸向黄昏去的路像一段灰心"，就明显流露出艾略特《普鲁弗洛克的情歌》中"街连着街，好象一场讨厌的争议……"的影响。

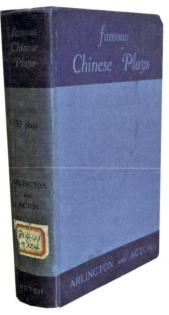

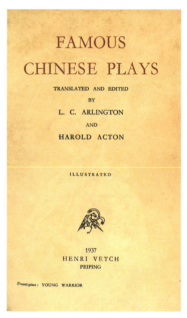

艾克敦参与编辑的《戏剧之精华》(沟通中西文化的见证)。

Famous Chinese Plays, translated and edited by L.C. Arlington and Harold Acton. Peiping：H. Vetch，1937.

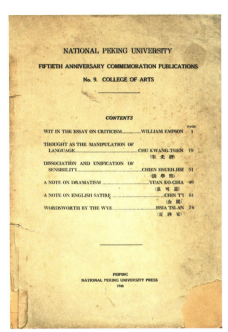

《国立北京大学五十周年纪念刊》第9号"文学院",收录燕卜荪论文《蒲柏〈批评论〉中的"慧"(Wit)》

National Peking University Fiftieth Anniversary Commemoration Publications, No. 9, 'College of Arts', Peking University Press, 1948

　　20世纪30年代,英国作家、学者哈罗德·艾克敦(Harold Acton,1904～1994)在北京大学讲授英国文学期间,也曾将《荒原》等英国现代诗作列为课文,并鼓励中国学生以艾略特为题写论文,培养了一批青年学子对现代诗的兴趣。另一位英国诗人、批评家燕卜荪(William Empson,1906～1984)在20世纪三四十年代也来到中国任教,抗战爆发后,他跟随临时大学(西南联大)从北平到长沙、蒙自、昆明,"同中国师生打成一片,彼此极为相得"[1],直接影响了穆旦、袁可嘉、王佐良等一代中国诗人和英国文学研究者。王佐良就曾回忆,燕卜荪的《当代英诗》课"从霍普金斯一直讲到奥登",讲解则是"书上找不到的内情、实况,加上他对于语言的精细分析"[2],令学生们大开眼界。

1　王佐良《谈穆旦的诗》,《王佐良文集》,外语教学与研究出版社,1997年,第429页。
2　王佐良《穆旦的由来与归宿》,《王佐良文集》,第466页。

王佐良《一个诗人的形成——〈哀里奥脱：诗人及批评家〉》，
《大公报·星期文艺》，1947年2月16日。
'The Formation of a Poet—Chapter I of *T.S. Eliot：the Poet
and Critic*' by Wang Zuoliang, *Ta Kung Pao*, Feb. 16, 1947.

钱学熙《T.S. 艾略脱 Eliot 批评思想体系的研
讨》，《学原》第二卷第五期，1948年。
'A Discussion on the System of T.S. Eliot's
Critical Thoughts' by Qian Xuexi, *Campus
Scientiae*, Vol. 2, No. 5, 1948.

　　王佐良晚年回忆，西南联大时期"我们都喜欢艾略特——除了《荒原》等诗，他的文论和他所主编的《标准》季刊也对我们有影响"[1]。抗战胜利之后，王佐良曾计划撰写一部艾略特评传，其中部分章节曾在天津《大公报·星期文艺》《文学周刊》发表。与此同时，袁可嘉除了在一系列论新诗现代化的论文中引述、评介艾略特的诗学理论之外，还曾撰文介绍国外最新出版的艾略特研究著作。1948 年，正在北大西语系任教的钱学熙则在《学原》杂志发表论文《T.S. 艾略脱 Eliot 批评思想体系的研讨》，根据艾略特本人的著作以及麦西生、李维斯、奈兹等英美学者的论述，从"诗底作用""诗底标准""写诗底条件""写诗底办法"等方面探讨了艾略特的批评理论。

1　王佐良《穆旦的由来与归宿》，《王佐良文集》，第 466 页。

　　20 世纪五六十年代，艾略特在中国内地遭到简单否定，却仍继续影响着港台地区的文学批评与创作。例如夏济安《香港——一九五〇》效仿《荒原》的"拼贴式"写法以及不同节律之间的对比，表现主人公从上海初到香港的印象和遭遇。1958 年在台北《文学杂志》发表时，夏济安撰写了长达数千字的后记，详细解释了创作背景、意图和字句含义。同期刊载的陈世骧的评介文章则认为夏济安这首诗所仿到的是"《荒原》背后的诗的传统意识之应用与活用"，"是一首相当重要的诗"。同时《文学杂志》还刊登了诗人卢飞白的《伦敦市上访艾略特——欧游杂诗之三》，记述了与艾略特会面的观感，"他从容得变成迟滞的言辞，/ 还带着浓厚的波士顿土味"等诗句活灵活现地勾勒出了这位大诗人的神态。此后卢飞白在芝加哥大学攻读博士学位期间，以艾略特为题撰写了学位论文《艾略特：他的诗论的辨证式的结构》，功力深厚，自成一家之言，1966 年由芝加哥大学出版社出版，成为中国学者最早在英美出版的艾略特研究专著之一。

夏济安《香港——一九五〇》，见《陈世骧文存》，辽宁教育出版社，1998 年。
Poem：'Hong Kong：Nineteen Fifty' by Hsia Tsi An（Xia Ji'an）.

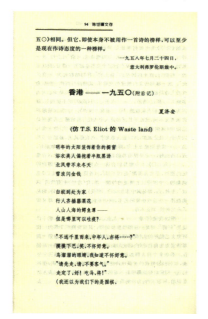
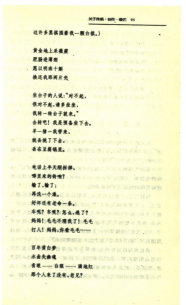

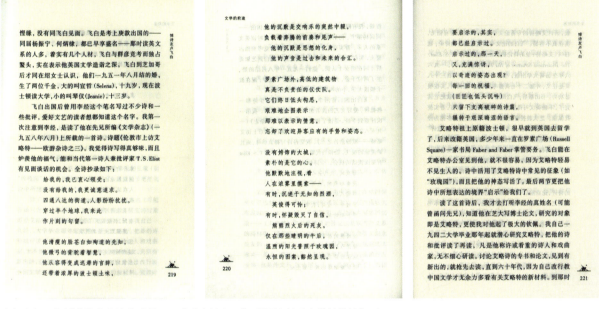

李经（卢飞白）《伦敦市上访艾略特——欧游杂诗之三》，见夏志清《文学的前途》，生活·读书·新知三联书店，2002年。
Poem：'A Meeting with T.S. Eliot in the City of London' by Lu Fei-Pai（Lu Feibai）.

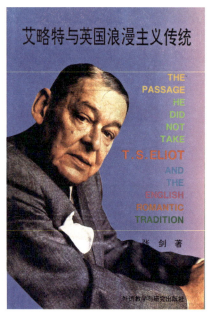  

张剑《艾略特与英国浪漫主义传统》，外语教学
与研究出版社，1996 年。
The Passage He Did Not Take：*T.S. Eliot
and the English Romantic Tradition* by Zhang
Jian, Foreign Language Teaching and
Research Press, 1996.

董洪川《"荒原"之风：T.S. 艾略特在中国》，北
京大学出版社，2004 年。
The Wind from 'the Waste Land'：*T.S.
Eliot in China* by Dong Hongchuan, Peking
University Press, 2004.

　　时至今日，艾略特对中国文坛的影响力依旧巨大，研究艾略特的专著层出不穷。其中既有从文艺创作角度进行探讨的研究，如张剑《艾略特与英国浪漫主义传统》、刘燕《现代批评之始：T.S. 艾略特诗学研究》、章晓宇《人文学视野下的 T.S. 艾略特诗学研究》、陈庆勋《艾略特诗歌隐喻研究》、郭磊《荒原问道：T.S. 艾略特诗歌的创伤主题研究》等，也有研究艾略特作品在中国的传播历程及其巨大影响的，如董洪川《"荒原"之风：T.S. 艾略特在中国》等。

专论

T.S. 艾略特："不朽的低语"

刘立平

  T.S. 艾略特 1888 年 9 月 26 日生于美国密苏里州的圣路易斯，父亲是个成功的企业家，母亲也颇有文学素养。他的祖父在圣路易斯建立了第一所唯一神教教会，并创建了华盛顿大学。1906 年，艾略特成为哈佛大学的学生，他不仅三年就获得了本科学位，而且在校期间还主编了文学刊物《哈佛呼声》杂志，他的诗才也在这时崭露头角。1910年，他获得了英国文学的硕士学位，之后去巴黎索邦大学学习了一年，回到哈佛后，他以 F.H. 布莱德利为研究对象开始攻读哲学的博士学位。1914 年，他获得奖学金，拟去德国的马尔堡大学学习，但是由于一战爆发，他只能去英国的牛津大学继续学业。在这里，艾略特结识了他人生中非常重要的一位人物：埃兹拉·庞德。此时，艾略特已经写成了《普鲁弗洛克的情歌》，可是一直没有发表的机会。在庞德的努力下，《诗刊》的编辑哈里特·门罗终于同意发表这首诗，并于 1915 年 6 月刊出。1916 年，艾略特完成了自己的博士论文，但是由于一战的缘故，他没能回到哈佛参加博士论文答辩，也没有得到他的博士学位。

  艾略特的第一本诗集《普鲁弗洛克及其他观察》1917 年在伦敦出版，第一版仅仅印刷了 500 册，而且四年后才销售出去。虽然诗集的销量不佳，艾略特却已经决心要成为一名作家。他的父母对此不以为然，希望艾略特能够回到美国，但是艾略特则认为欧洲代表着文学的传统，若想成为一名伟大的作家，必须生活在欧洲，为此他违背了父母的意愿，决心留在伦敦。在这期间他不得不找各种工作来贴补自己的生活。艾略特先后做过教师、银行职员和编辑等工作。他创办了一本重要的文学季刊《标准》，并长期担任主编。1925 年，他成为费柏出版社的编辑，并且帮助其成为英国最有名的出版社之一。1927 年，他入了英国的国教，同时加入英国国籍。1948 年，他获得诺贝尔文学奖，达到了声誉的顶峰。

  在亚瑟·阿蒙斯的《文学中的象征主义运动》一书中，艾略特开始接触法国象征主义作家兰波、魏尔伦和拉弗格等人。艾略特意识到，诗歌不仅可以描写乡村以外的城市，而且还可以描写城市肮脏、丑陋的一面。诗人可以完全摒弃浪漫主义那种滥情，在诗中呈现一种戏剧化的场景，他将这些学到的技巧运用到了他的早期诗歌《普鲁弗洛克的情歌》当中。这首诗虽然名字叫做"情歌"，却没有热烈的追求或失恋的悲伤，而是一个有点自卑和神经质的叙述者的戏剧独白。在浪漫主义诗歌中出现的美丽的黄昏在这里则给人一种冰冷、麻木、不安的感觉。整首诗语气迟缓、冷漠、疲惫、犹豫。普鲁弗洛克是个虚构的人物，他既不是预言家（拉萨路），也不是悲剧式的英雄（哈姆雷特），他觉得他最好的年华已经逝去；他害怕生活；他没有勇气也没有能力与他心仪的女性交流，他是一个没有行动能力的反英雄。这首诗貌似一首叙事诗，但是既没有具体的人物，也没有具体的情节，整首诗都在解答一个不断重复，无法解答的问题。这首诗也没有一个具体的地点，这个故事可能发生在任何一个现代城市（巴黎、伦敦或圣路易斯）。普鲁弗洛克也不是一个真正的人物，只是流动的、碎片化的意识。这首诗与美国当时的诗歌风格完全不同，被认为是"惠特曼和狄金森之后最有原创性的诗歌"。

《荒原》是 20 世纪最著名的长诗。写于 1921 年，庞德对此诗进行了大幅修改，1922 年 10 月出版于《标准》杂志。这首诗写得非常消极，这与作者的生活背景不无关系，这时一战刚刚结束，战争给这一代的诗人带来了巨大的心理创伤。艾略特同时经历了一次非常不幸的婚姻，他因此而神经崩溃，而这首诗的创作前后，他正处于恢复期。

《荒原》晦涩难懂，诗中描述的是一个缺乏信仰、爱与希望的世界。虽然艾略特说，这首诗是"个人对于生活无足轻重的牢骚"，但实际上却是对现代文明的批判。除了形式上的支离破碎，整首诗还运用了七种外语以及 37 处之多的用典。其中所涉及的两本人类学著作尤其重要：一是杰西·韦斯顿的《从仪式到传奇》，二是詹姆斯·弗雷泽的《金枝》。这里主要包括两个故事，一个是亚瑟王寻找圣杯的故事，另外一个就是鱼王的故事，这两个故事包括了诗歌的最主要的论题：死亡与再生。《荒原》共分五个部分：《死者葬仪》《对弈》《火诫》《水里的死亡》和《雷霆所说的》。这五部分如同传统的五幕剧，节奏的变化有点类似爵士乐。诗歌中出现了不同阶层人物的声音。有高雅的语言，也有粗俗的语言；有对话，也有歌剧风格的歌曲；既有荒凉的不毛之地，也有再生和繁殖的意象。第一部分《死者葬仪》原指英国国教祈祷书中的葬礼仪式，这里可能指一战中死去的人，或者鱼王之死，或者进一步引申到西方文明之死。这里出现的意象是枯死的树、没有流水声音的岩石和"并无实体的城。"第二部分《对弈》则更多涉及堕胎、强暴、性无能等"不幸或不正常的两性关系"。第三部分《火诫》中出现了一个现代女人的形象，她不想死，但是她对自己和周围的漠然态度却代表了生命的死亡。第四部分《水里的死亡》同样涉及情欲，但是情欲带来的却是灾难，因为情欲的大海能将人淹死。第五部分《雷霆的话》给出了解决方案：给予、慈悲和克制。给予是欲望的对立面，要放弃自己的小我；慈悲可以让人舍己为人；克制能够帮助我们控制欲望，净化欲望使之变成精神之火。

其实除了《荒原》这首长诗，艾略特还写过一些非常有影响的诗歌，如《空心人》《圣灰星期三》《四个四重奏》等。《四个四重奏》发表于 1943 年，艾略特本人认为这是他最好的作品。在创作这首诗的时候，艾略特愈发认同英国文化和价值观。此诗的四节，有三节都发生在英国，涉及英国的历史。每一节的标题都使用了一个地名。第一节为"焚毁的诺顿"，是英国格罗斯特郡的玫瑰花园；第二节为"东科克尔村"，这是萨默赛特的一个村庄，艾略特的祖先安德鲁·艾略特曾经在此寻找宗教的自由；第三节为"干燥的塞尔维吉斯"，讲的是圣路易斯密苏里附近的密西西比河和新英格兰的海滨；最后一小节为"小吉丁"，发生地点是 17 世纪英国国教社区建立的英国的村庄。

这首诗的每一节都可独立成诗，每一节都是一个四重奏，包括五个"乐章"。诗歌中出现了空气、土、水、火四元素和四个季节，每一小节对应一个元素。在这首诗中，艾略特"探索着时间和永恒，赎罪与得救，人生与自然，人生与历史，诗与语言等等问题，最后统归于基督教义，从中得到了归宿，得到了矛盾和对立的混一的境界。"

艾略特还是一个重要的批评家。他在《传统与个人才能》及《论玄学派诗人》等文章中所提出的"非个性论"、"客观对应物"等概念也得到了很多诗人的推崇。1920 年，艾略特出版了他的第一本批评文集《圣林》，里面包括了艾略特最重要的一篇批评文章《传统与个人才能》。虽然他描述自己是"政治上的保皇派，文学上的古典主义者，宗教上是英国天主教徒"，但实际上他既强调传统，也重视创新。他认为诗歌传统具有连续性，在某种程度上没有巨大的改变，但他同时认为个人才能可以重构传统，可以让人从另一个角度重新审视传统。"现存的艺术经典本身就构成一个理想的秩序，这个秩序由于新的（真正新的）作品被介绍进来而发生变化。这个已成的秩序在新作品出现以前本是完整的，加入新花样以后要继续保持完整，整个的秩序就必须改变一下，即使改变得很小。"因此在个人才能遭遇传统的时候，要放弃自己的个性，放弃个人的喜怒哀乐，进入一个超越自身的广阔领域。但是传统本身是个整体，要进入这个系统就必须要改变它。除了诗歌和评论外，他还是一位剧作家，创作了《大教堂谋杀案》《合家团聚》《机要秘书》《政界元老》和《鸡尾酒会》等作品，展现了自己多方面的才华。

1965 年 1 月 4 日，艾略特去世，应他的要求，他的骨灰被埋在英国的东科克尔村，这是他的祖先安德鲁·艾略特曾经生活的地方。他的墓碑上写着《四个四重奏》中"东科克尔克村"的第一句和最后一句："我的开始就是我的终点，我的终点就是我的开始。"

刘立平

天津外国语大学副教授，北京外国语大学文学博士，美国宾夕法尼亚大学访问学者。主要从事英美诗歌研究。

T.S. ELIOT: 'WHISPERS OF IMMORTALITY'

Liu Liping

Thomas Stearns Eliot was born on September 26 1888 in St Louis, Missouri, U.S.A. His father was a successful industrialist, and his mother had a great love of literature. His grandfather founded both the first Unitarian church in St. Louis and Washington University. In 1906, Eliot entered Harvard University, where he not only obtained his bachelor's degree, but was also the chief editor of *The Harvard Advocate*, in which some of his poems were published. In 1910, he received a master's degree in English literature and then went to the Sorbonne, in Paris, for a year. After that he returned to Harvard to begin doctoral work on the philosophy of F.H. Bradley. Meanwhile he won a fellowship to study at Marburg University, in Germany, yet with the outbreak of World War I, he was forced to continue his studies at Oxford University. In England, Eliot met Ezra Pound, who would become one of the most important figures in his life. At that time, Eliot had written 'The Love Song of J. Alfred Prufrock', but nobody would publish it. Through Pound's efforts, *Poetry* magazine editor Harriet Monroe, finally agreed to publish the poem in June 1915. In 1916, Eliot finished his doctoral dissertation, but he was unable to return to Harvard due to the war. Hence, he didn't defend the thesis and obtain his doctorate.

Eliot's first volume of poems, *Prufrock and Other Observations*, was published in London in 1917. The 500 copies of the first edition took four years to sell out. Despite this, Eliot determined to become a writer, yet his parents disapproved and hoped Eliot would return to America. Believing that Europe better represented the tradition of literature and one must live there if he wanted to become a great writer, Eliot went against his parents' wishes and settled in London. However, he had to find various jobs to make ends meet. He became a teacher, a bank clerk and an editor successively. He founded a literary quarterly *The Criterion* and became the chief editor for a long time. In 1925, Eliot joined the Faber & Gwyer (later Faber & Faber), which would later become one of the most renowned publishers in the country thanks to his efforts. Eliot was baptized into the Anglican Church, and became a British citizen in 1927. In 1948, Eliot reached the pinnacle of his fame when he was awarded the Nobel Prize for Literature.

It was through Arthur Symons' *The Symbolist Movement in Literature* that Eliot became familiar with the work of French symbolists such as Arthur Rimbaud, Paul Verlaine, and Jules Laforgue. Eliot realized that other than the countryside, it was also possible to present the sordid, filthy metropolis in poetry. Poets could discard the sentimentality of Romanticism and convey a dramatic setting in a poem. He applied these techniques into his early poem 'The Love Song of J. Alfred Prufrock'. There is no passionate pursuit or broken-hearted sadness in this so-called 'love song', but instead a dramatic monologue of a self-debased neurotic. The beautiful evening often described in romantic poems becomes cold, numb and disturbing in Eliot's poem. The tone is dilatory, indifferent, tired and hesitant. Prufrock is a fictional character who was neither a prophet (John the Baptist) nor a tragic hero (Hamlet). He felt his best years had passed and he was scared to live. He lacked courage and ability to converse with his object of affection. In other words, he was an incapable anti-hero. It takes the form of a narrative poem yet there is no specific character or concrete plot. It seems to ask a repetitive, unanswered question throughout. Furthermore, the poem does not have a specific geographical setting. It could depict any modern city, be it Paris, London or St Louis. Prufrock is not a real character, and is merely representative of the mobile, fragmented consciousness. This poem is completely different from the popular style in the U.S. at the time, and it is believed to be 'the most obviously original poem since the works of Walt Whitman and Emily Dickinson'.[1]

The Waste Land, one of the most famous poems in the 20th century, was written by Eliot in 1921 and heavily revised by Ezra Pound. It was published in *The Criterion* in October 1922. The profoundly depressing poem bore close relation to Eliot's life: at that time, World War I had just ended, which caused immense psychological trauma to the poets of the generation. Eliot had gone through an unfortunate marriage which caused him to suffer a nervous breakdown. The poem was written around a period of convalescence.

The Waste Land is obscure and difficult, portraying a world without love, hope and faith. Eliot said that it was 'only the relief of a personal and insignificant grouse against life', but it was also actually a critique of modern civilization. In addition to broken forms, the poem contains at least 37 allusions and quotations in seven languages. Two books of anthropology were especially

---

1 Christopher Beach, *The Cambridge Introduction to Twentieth-Century American Poetry*, New York: Cambridge University Press, 2003, p. 37.

important: *From Ritual to Romance* by Jessie Weston, and *The Golden Bough* by James Frazer. Two stories were included: Arthurian quest for the Holy Grail, and the story of the Fisher King. They comprise the foremost topic of this poem: death and resurrection. *The Waste Land* includes five parts: 'The Burial of the Dead', 'A Game of Chess', 'The Fire Sermon', 'Death by Water', and 'What the Thunder Said'. The five sections are structured like a traditional play in five acts. The diverse rhythm reads like jazz music. The voices of different characters represent various classes. Refined language mingles with rough language; dialogues interweave with opera-style songs; image of deserted land blends with image of fertility. The first part 'The Burial of the Dead' originally refers to the burial ritual in the Anglican Church, and it may allude to the dead in World War I or the death of Fisher King, or the death of western civilization by extension. It contains the images of a dead tree, a dry stone without sound of water and an 'unreal city'. The second part 'A Game of Chess' relates to 'unfortunate or abnormal sexual relationships like abortion, violence, and impotency.'[1] In part three, an image of a modern woman appears. She does not want to die while her indifferent attitude to her surroundings represents her spiritual death. The fourth part, 'Death in Water', involves erotic desire. Nevertheless, this desire brings disaster, for the sea of erotic desire can drown human beings. The fifth part 'What the Thunder said' gives a solution, that is, 'datta' (give), 'dayadhvam' (sympathize), 'damyata' (control). To give is the opposite of desire which requires a person to give up oneself. Sympathy means sacrificing one's own interests for the sake of others; control will help us regulate and purify our desire so that desire can change into spiritual fire.

In addition to *The Waste Land*, Eliot also wrote some other very influential poems such as 'The Hollow Man', 'Ash Wednesday' and 'Four Quartets'. 'Four Quartets' was published in 1943, and was considered by Eliot as his best work. Eliot identified intensely with British culture and its values during the time of writing this poem, in which three of four sections relate to Britain and touch on British history. The title of each section is a landmark. The first section is called 'Burnt Norton', which is a rose garden in Gloucestershire. The second part, 'East Coker', is a village in Somerset, where Eliot's ancestor, Andrew Eliot, sought religious freedom. The third quartet, 'The Dry Salvages', is about the Mississippi River in St Louis, Missouri, and the New England seaside. The last part, 'Little Gidding', is a village founded by an Anglican religious community in the 17th century.

1　T.S. Eliot, *The Waste Land*. Trans. by Zhao Luorui & Zhang Ziqing. Beijing: Yanshan Publishing House, 2006, p. 74.

Each section is a separate poem and a 'quartet' with five 'movements' in it. The quartets are structured by the four elements (air, earth, water, and fire) and four seasons. Each part corresponds to one element. In this poem, Eliot 'explores a lot of questions: time and eternity, redemption and salvation, life and nature, life and history, and poetry and language, etc. All problems could be solved by Christian doctrine. People could find comfort and peace from it, hence eliminate contradiction and opposition'.[1]

Eliot was also an important critic. He put forward concepts like 'impersonality', 'objective correlative' and his work is revered by many poets. In 1920, Eliot published his first volume of criticism *The Sacred Wood*, which included 'Tradition and Individual Talent'. It is often considered his most important essay. Though he described himself as a 'royalist in politics, classicist in literature, and Anglo-Catholic in religion', he actually emphasized the importance of both tradition and innovation. He believed there was succession in the tradition of poetry, and that tradition does not transform itself to some extent; nonetheless, he also thought that individual talent could reconstitute tradition and help reexamine tradition from different perspectives. 'The existing monuments form an ideal order among themselves which is modified by the introduction of the new (the really new) work of art among them. The existing order is complete before the new work arrives; for order to persist after the supervention of novelty, the whole existing order must be, if ever so slightly, altered.'[2] If individual talent confronts tradition, you should abandon your personality and your personal emotions and enter a vast sphere beyond yourself. Tradition is a whole, into which you have to alter it. Eliot was not only a poet and critic, but also a playwright. He wrote several plays such as *Murder in the Cathedral*, *The Family Reunion*, *The Confidential Clerk*, *The Elder Statesman*, and *The Cocktail Party*, demonstrating his talent in many different literary formats.

Eliot died on January 4 1965. At his request, his ashes were buried in East Coker, England, where his ancestor Andrew Eliot had once lived. On his tombstone, the first and last lines from the 'East Coker' were inscribed: 'In my beginning is my end' and 'In my end is my beginning'.

---

1   Zhou Jueliang, *Selected Works of Zhou Jueliang*. Beijing: Foreign Language Teaching and Research Press, 2011. p. 55.

2   David H. Richter, *The Critical Tradition: Classic Texts and Contemporary Trends*, New York: Bedford/St. Martin's, 2007, p. 538.

Liu Liping

An associate professor of English at Tianjin Foreign Studies University. He received his doctorate in literature at Beijing Foreign Studies University, and was a visiting scholar at the University of Pennsylvania. His areas of research include British and American poetry.